A
PSYCHOTHERAPIST'S
DARK JOURNEY INTO
THE SUICIDAL MIND

A
PSYCHOTHERAPIST'S
DARK JOURNEY INTO
THE SUICIDAL MIND

◆

A Relationship Approach to
Understanding and Healing

Ronald L. Bonner, Psy.D.

iUniverse, Inc.
New York Lincoln Shanghai

A PSYCHOTHERAPIST'S DARK JOURNEY INTO THE SUICIDAL MIND

A Relationship Approach to Understanding and Healing

iUniverse books may be ordered through booksellers or by contacting:

iUniverse
2021 Pine Lake Road, Suite 100
Lincoln, NE 68512
www.iuniverse.com
1-800-Authors (1-800-288-4677)

ISBN-13: 978-0-595-35484-9 (pbk)
ISBN-13: 978-0-595-79976-3 (ebk)
ISBN-10: 0-595-35484-X (pbk)
ISBN-10: 0-595-79976-0 (ebk)

Printed in the United States of America

IN MEMORY OF

My father, James J. Bonner (1914–1990), whose life consumed too much of the dark journey. Like it or not, after all these years, you continue to drive me toward the dark journey and wanting to understand more. I hope you have found peace.

My good friend, teacher, and healer, Sr. Noel Mattes, OSF (1942–1989), whose life radiated all that is good about living. Even in your darkest moments, including suffering and dying from terminal cancer, you remained an ever radiant light to those hurting and in darkness.

"I HAVE A DREAM"

I have a dream, a song to sing. To help me cope with anything. If you see the wonder of a fairy tale, you can take the future even if you fail. I believe in angels, something good in everything I see. I believe in angels when I know the time is right for me. I'll cross the stream, I have a dream. I have a dream, a fantasy to help me through reality. And my destination makes it worth the while. Pushing through the darkness still another mile. I believe in angels, something good in everything I see, I believe in angels when I know the time is right for me. I'll cross the stream, I have a dream.

—By Benny Anderson and Bjorn Ulvaeus

—Sr. Noel's favorite life song of hope

Contents

Acknowledgments

God knows I have been blessed to have so many good people along the journey, who in one way or another are responsible for the ideas in this work. From the beginning, my sister and brother-in-law, Judith and Austin Mallozzi, who took over my child rearing, after the death of my mother and ongoing dark journey of my father: you were and are my parents. You provided me with love, nurturing, and guidance, which continue to help me find the way. For so many good people of faith in the middle years, including Fr. Gus Milon, Sr. Gus Taurish, Sr. Noel Mattes, Mr. George Walter, Fr. Harold Parsons, Children of Yahweh, Faith-in-Action-Today Youth Group, and all the spirit-filled communities, thank you for being my beacons of light. You profoundly touched my soul and gave me some of the very best reasons for living. For my very special friend from early on, Ms. Mary Hamilton: because of you I better understand faith, the power of attachments, and the suffering that goes along with their loss. You are a wonderful soul who will never be forgotten. And to another special friend, Dennis Fall, who perhaps understood my mind better than anyone: I thank you for accepting and validating my sometimes dark journey and pushing me to become a healer. I am so sorry that I let us go.

Thank you, Dr. Aylene Harper, for turning me on to psychology. In one way or another, I am here because of you. To my mentor, research partner, and good friend, Dr. Alex Rich: thank you so much for believing in me and conceptualizing, supporting, and joining the research of the dark journey, in spite of the misgivings and myths held by our social psychologist colleagues on the research ethics committee. We sure have had a great history together. For the past, present, and future of clinical suicidology, Dr. Edwin Shneidman stands above all others in understanding and helping people on the dark journey. You have been the father to many of us who have tried to better understand and help those who suffer the unbearable emotional pain, the psychache, of the dark journey. Thank you for giving us the heart and soul of the relationship work. I also am indebted to my "jailbird friends and leaders," Pastor Doug Schader, Dr. Jim Davison, Mr. Dennis Hammond, Associate Warden Tom Szulanczyk, Warden Mike Zenk, Ms. Denielle Thomas, and Ms. Lisa Edinger, who have greatly brightened my life behind bars and made doing time much easier. A special thanks go to Jim and Dennis who have rekindled the adolescent in me—"Three for one, three for all." From the beginning, through now, and to the end, I am so lucky to have the very best friend, Mr. Fred Bercik, stand by me through the ups and downs and the light and dark journeys. You have been the constant source of companionship that has helped me through it all. Thank you, Big Bubba. To my greatest gifts, Diane, Jason, and Joshua: you have been the very best reasons for living. You light my way, even when my mind drifts toward work and the dark journey of the suicidal mind. How lucky I have been! Finally, to every suicidal person who has allowed me to join them on the dark journey, you have been my best teachers, and I will never be the same. I wish you Noel's life song of hope today and tomorrow.

Disclaimer

This book does not offer formal training for psychotherapists or direct specific treatment for suicidal persons. Expert advice, training, and consultation should be sought from competent professionals for these areas.

Introduction

There are a variety of books in the suicidology and psychotherapy fields that deal with specific assessment and therapy techniques in working with suicidal people. Measurement instruments, structured treatment plans, and step-by-step therapy programs are now available to assist psychotherapists in this work. Suicidology literature has greatly advanced to include a wealth of information on theories of suicide, causes of suicide, population profiles, and risk factors. Clinical training programs for suicide risk assessment and treatment have finally started to develop. Much of what exists for the psychotherapist remains static and piecemeal and has historically taken a learn-as-you-go approach. The purpose of this work is to provide an organizing framework within a relationship approach for the therapist working with suicidal people. The ideas in this work may prove useful to all helpers, including psychologists, psychiatrists, mental health counselors, social workers, and pastoral counselors, who wish to understand and heal the dark journey of the suicidal person through the helping relationship. The metaphor of the dark journey of the suicidal mind was chosen for several reasons, including the developmental life process of the suicide idea, the dark state of the suicidal mind, dark mind state ideas, dark emotions, dark psychache and physiology, dark stress and coping processes, and finally the dark life story of the suicidal person.

The thesis of this work is that, to be effective, the psychotherapist must join the suicidal person on the dark journey, understand from the person's experience how the idea of suicide has come to make "sense," and finally affirm and validate the suicide journey. In so doing, the psychotherapist builds a healing relationship that can offer hope, relief, and skills to redirect the dark journey of the suicidal person to one of light, possibilities, and life.

This book was written from the perspective of a psychotherapist working with suicidal adults on an outpatient basis. It generally does not apply to children, adolescents, or people in acute crises who need psychiatric hospitalization; these are situations that present somewhat different dynamics. It also does not apply to such suicide variants as rational suicide, suicide-homicide-hostage situations, suicide terrorist actions, suicide by cop scenarios, or indirect paths of self-destruction. The book is for the psychotherapist working with the suicidal person who has been on a life journey of darkness, which includes the suicide idea, psychache, and hopelessness. The thoughts that follow are the culminations of personal experience, clinical experience, and research, but do not substitute in any way for the unique clinical picture of each person on the dark journey and the clinical judgment and professional consultation needed in developing and implementing a treatment plan of healing.

1

The Dark Suicide Idea

Some thirty-five years ago, I tried desperately to speak to my father's psychiatrist after my father had again been hospitalized for depression. Once the psychiatrist finally accepted the call, I asked him what was wrong with my father and whether and why my father wanted to kill himself. He responded with no emotion, "Your father is ill. He has a chemical imbalance. That's all I can tell you." These words were hardly comforting to a ten-year-old who was very worried about his father.

Today, I sit with family members who have had a loved one die by suicide. They always ask me why he or she did it. I also sit with many who live with the suicide idea. Ironically, they never ask why, but instead want to know how and if they can ever feel better. Like the psychiatrist, I, too, have told family members and suicidal people about chemical imbalances and the whole host of risk factors, to include depression, family disorganization, cognitive distortions, suicide genes, serotonin deficiencies, suicide models, chronic and acute stress, and physical and emotional pain. In terms of trying to help suicidal people feel better, I have administered a number of assessment devices to measure these factors and implemented various therapy techniques to try to improve these dynamics. I also have educated suicidal people on the latest research on suicide, its causes, and treatments. In spite of these efforts, as a psychotherapist, I have often felt the void I felt as a child when talking to my father's psychiatrist, of not really getting at the right questions or the right answers to help the suicidal person. My fear is that I have too often left people on the dark journey in the dark when it comes to relief and recovery.

The dilemma takes me back to the days of my doctoral dissertation on college student suicide. It began with a quote from the renowned poet Anne Sexton, whose life captured the dark journey of the suicide idea. She constantly struggled with pervasive thoughts, ruminations, and plans of killing herself, until one day she finally succeeded.

> Since you ask, most days I cannot remember.
> I walk in my clothing, unmasked by that voyage.
> Then the almost unbearable lust returns.
> Even then I have nothing against life.
> I know well the grass blades you mention,
> the furniture you have placed under the sun.
> But suicides have a special language.
> Like carpenters, they want to know which tools.
> They never ask why build.

—Anne Sexton: "Wanting to Die," cited in Hendin, 1993

The question "why" seems to serve little purpose for the suicidal person. Reframing the question as to how the dark journey progresses and retreats would seem to offer understanding and hope for the suicidal person.

The dark journey reflects a life process that is dark and blinding, wherein light, answers, relief, and hope are unable to be seen or obtained. As I sit with people with the suicide idea, I often will take a minute, close my eyes, and imagine being in a cold cave of total darkness with no ideas or clues to where the light or opening might be. I can imagine myself trying to maneuver my way only to bump into things or trip and fall, becoming increasingly frustrated and injured. I can also imagine that, if I was left in this cave of total darkness for hours, days, weeks, or months, my physical and psychological needs would become severely thwarted, my body and mind would eventually break down, and despair and hopelessness would consume my being. And so it is with the dark journey into the suicidal mind.

According to Kral (1994, p. 245):

[S]uicide is caused by the idea of suicide and nothing else. It is a conscious option to kill oneself made by the individual, almost always to escape from unbearable, psychological pain, or as Shneidman (1993) has recently put it, from unbearable "psych-ache."

The suicide idea comprises a process of stages that include passive suicide ideation, contemplation of the benefits and costs of suicide, suicidal decision making and planning, and finally the behavioral response of suicide action (Bonner, 2005a, 2005b, 2001; Bonner & Rich, 1992, 1988a; Rich & Bonner, 1990). The suicide idea begins with passive suicide ideation that is fleeting. It is often triggered by some negative life event, such as situational stress, a life problem, or a developmental impasse. Passive suicide ideation provides a brief mental escape in the event that the trigger was not resolved.

However, some people who encounter more triggers, upsetting affect, and uncertainty about problem resolution will progress to the second stage, suicide contemplation. It is at this point that the suicide idea takes on a life of its own, where it becomes more pervasive and intense, and the person seriously thinks about suicide and the associated costs and benefits. For most people at this stage who have problem resolution and affect relief, the costs outweigh the benefits of suicide, and they retreat from the suicide idea. For others, however, whose problems persist and emotional suffering worsens, the stage of suicidal decision making and planning will occur. At this point, the suicide idea becomes all consuming and highly valued as a "reasonable" solution to life problems. The person at this stage makes the decision to attempt suicide and plans and acquires a method for implementation. While the person at this stage becomes fully prepared for suicide action (e.g., method, suicide note, giving away possessions, writing a will, etc.), he or she may not do so depending on his or her level of and threshold for emotional pain. It is when this individual threshold is met that the person will be driven into the final stage of suicide action, as a desperate attempt to obtain relief and escape from intolerable emotional pain.

Aaron Beck and colleagues (e.g., Beck, Kovacs, & Weissman, 1979; Beck & Lester, 1976; Beck, Schuyler & Herman, 1974; Weishaar & Beck, 1992) have spent many years studying the components of the suicide idea. The Scale for Suicide Ideation was developed to assess the degree to which a person is thinking about suicide. The suicide idea is examined in relation to frequency and duration, the ability to control suicide wishes, the characteristics of the contemplated attempt (preparation and final acts), the purpose of the contemplated attempt, the availability and opportunity of the method, and the relative strength of the person's wish to live and wish to die.

For the person who has carried the suicide idea through to action, these researchers also developed the Suicide Intent Scale to help the therapist determine the severity of a person's psychological intent to die at the time of the suicide attempt. This measure taps the attempter's thoughts and behaviors before, during, and after the attempt, including the purpose of the attempt, attitudes toward living and dying, and relationship of drug and alcohol usage to the suicide attempt.

In terms of the psychotherapist identifying the stage and components of the suicide idea, the person's history is considered critical in anticipating future suicide ideas and action, given certain life event cues or triggers. Past suicidal behavior is the best predictor of future suicidal behavior. The suicide idea is at the core of the person's dark journey, and for some people it becomes a self-maintaining cycle that repeats itself and flourishes over time to culminate in eventual suicide. By the suicidal person's invitation and the psychotherapist's acceptance, validation, and systematic exploration of the suicide idea and its history, the dark journey can become permeable to light, hope, and change. This process is extremely difficult and time consuming. An intimate therapeutic relationship must develop over time in which the suicidal person comes to trust the therapist and openly welcomes the therapist into his or her dark journey of the suicide idea. This step is very risky for the suicidal person, as the therapist, like others, may invalidate the journey even out of good intention. The therapist may negate, minimize, label, involuntarily commit, psychoanalyze, abandon, or challenge by pointing out how good the person has it compared to others or telling the person to just snap out of it and start thinking about others. These responses undermine the suicide journey and minimize the emotional pain, causing the suicidal person to hurt further and retreat deeper into the suicide idea.

In terms of accepting, validating, and working with the suicide idea, I am reminded of an interview I had many years ago with a psychologist who owned a private practice. When asked about my clinical interests, I shared about my interest in working with suicidal people. She quickly responded, "I really don't deal with suicide—it's a cop-out—it's about something else—not gonna reward a patient for suicide!" Being young, naive, and wanting the job, I am sorry to say I did not tell her what I really thought. While a psychotherapist may rightfully choose not to work with someone on the dark journey of suicide and thereby make appropriate referrals, the psychotherapeutic work is fundamentally, directly, and systematically about suicide. The psychotherapist's primary job is to understand, empathize, and validate the suicide idea and how it makes perfect experiential sense for the person on the dark journey. The suicide idea is the core of the dark journey and ties all of the pieces of the life story together. The work is intense, anxiety-provoking, sometimes depressing, and dark, and psychotherapists may find themselves deeply affected by the journey. For psychotherapists who choose the work and take the journey, there is no greater reward than to see a life stricken with emotional pain, anguish, darkness, and death transformed into a new path of light, hope, and possibility.

2

Other Dark Suicide Ideas

One of the primary ways the suicide idea develops is through the activation of other dark, self-defeating suicide ideas along the journey. In describing this process, Shneidman (1998) paraphrased the Bard as follows: "…the mind's the site to catch each suicide in its flight (p. 250)."

To revisit the metaphor of darkness, the suicidal person is trapped in a cold, dark cave of total darkness where light or an exit cannot be found. Over time, this becomes an extremely frightening experience and suicide comes to be seen as the only way out of a terribly bleak existence. A number of pro-suicide ideas have been identified that contribute to, reinforce, and maintain the dark journey.

Hopelessness, or negative future expectations, is considered a core element of the suicidal mind. The person is unable to see light, relief, or problem resolution in the future. The person not only sees a current dark existence but sees only more darkness and emotional pain down the road. Aaron Beck's research team has spent the last four decades researching hopelessness and finding its primary role in suicide ideation, suicide attempts, and suicide completions (e.g., Beck, 1996, 1986, 1976; Beck, Steer, Kovacs, & Garrison, 1985; Beck, Steer, & Brown, 1993; Warman, Forman, Henriques, Brown, & Beck, 2004). Hopelessness fuels the dark journey and eventually drives the person into despair and suicide action. The psychotherapist must understand and accept the person's hopeless state of mind, while simultaneously providing a validating experience that offers hope and possibilities for relief and problem resolution. The psychotherapist becomes the personification of hope in the midst of darkness and despair.

Pro-suicide beliefs also compose the dark journey and blind the suicidal person from seeing light, possibilities, and hope (Ellis & Newman, 1996). Some of the core common pro-suicide beliefs follow.

-Others will be better off without me.

-I can't take any more of the pain.

-The future is only going to get worse.

-Without her/him, I have nothing for which to live.

-I am too much of a burden to my family.

-At least I'll be out of here when I die.

-Nobody really cares whether I'm dead or alive.

-Killing myself will show others how I felt!

-Death will bring me peace; there will be no more problems.

-It's my life; I can kill myself if I want to!

—(Bonner, 2005a)

In identifying these common suicide beliefs, the psychotherapist needs to engage the person in dialogue to determine how suicide has come to make "sense" by ascription to these beliefs. The therapist accepts these beliefs as possibilities but gently encourages the suicidal person to examine the evidence, test the belief empirically, and consider alternative beliefs or ways of thinking. Chapter 6 reviews specific dialogic techniques that can shift, dispute, disrupt, and modify pro-suicide beliefs. Such therapeutic tactics are implemented within the context of an intimate, therapeutic, validating relationship.

Another common dark suicide idea has to do with the suicide fantasy. People on the dark journey often have a fantasy about what suicide will do, what effects it will have on others, and what, if any, efforts others will make to try to rescue them (Bonner, 2005a, 2001). When angry with others, these people often fantasize about suicide as a retaliation that will make others feel upset and guilty. For those in emotional pain or who are dealing with an "unsolvable" problem, the fantasy depicts relief, escape, and peace. Often the psychotherapist becomes a central part of the fantasy. Maltsberger and Buie (1973) caution therapists to be very careful with "countertransference hate," which develops out of the therapist's anxiety, depression, or anger toward the person who holds on to the suicide idea. Psychotherapists often feel controlled by suicidal people and come to resent their own dependency, the suicidal person's dependency, continual crisis calls, and the ultimate control the person always has in choosing to kill himself or herself. Fears of survivor guilt as well as malpractice litigation compound these issues for the psychotherapist, who must be keenly in touch with his or her feelings and reactions to the suicidal person. According to Shneidman, "the transference and countertransference…can legitimately be much more intense and more deep than would seemingly or appropriately (or even ethically) be in ordinary psychotherapy (1993, p. 141)." Again, the psychotherapist must remain the beacon of light for the suicidal person in the dark mental cave and not allow countertransference reactions to play out in the therapeutic relationship. While self-disclosure of some of these fears may be useful in the context of a validating relationship, the therapist's stance must remain one of compassion, understanding, and hope for the suicidal mind.

When ready, the suicidal person must examine the suicide fantasy in terms of narcissistic needs, the probable reality outcome, and the likely effects on others. The suicidal person will also need encouragement to examine how the suicide fantasy may in fact sabotage interpersonal relationships and minimize the actual kindness and support others have shown, including the therapy relationship. In time, the psychotherapist must gently confront the unreality of the suicide fantasy and clarify what the person's suicide may actually do and not do.

The dark journey of the suicidal mind is a desperate attempt to solve problems of living. Research has shown that suicidal people lack problem-solving skills, making them unprepared to think flexibly and generate or implement solutions necessary for successful problem-solving and adaptive coping (Clum & Febbraro, 2004). Suicide ideators have been shown to be unable to generate relevant alternatives to problem-solving scenarios (Schotte & Clum, 1982); attempters have been found to identify more negative consequences for their solutions and provide more irrelevant alternatives, and they were less likely to implement identified solutions (Schotte & Clum, 1987). Other studies have shown suicide ideators and attempters to have significantly lower levels of problem-solving confidence (Bonner & Rich, 1992, 1988a, 1987; Clum & Febbraro, 2004; Rudd, Rajeb, & Dahm, 1994), which was found to be strongly associated with hopelessness, independent of a depressed mood (Bonner & Rich, 1992, 1991, 1988b). While the exact role of problem-solving in suicidality remains unclear (in terms of what causes what), the therapist on the journey should help the suicidal person examine problems objectively and work as a coach in helping the person generate and implement solutions to life problems. Successful experiences and validation coaching will help the suicidal person develop problem-solving confidence in his or her self and open up his or her mind to possibilities.

Marsha Linehan and associates (e.g., Linehan 1999, 1985; Linehan, Goodstein, Nielson, & Chiles, 1983; Linehan, Camper, & Chiles Strosahl, & Shearin, 1987) have studied the concept of adaptive beliefs or reasons for living that protect and direct people away from the dark journey of the suicidal mind. What are those beliefs that help keep people coping and going when in the midst of stress and the problems of living? Some of the common reasons for living have to do with children, family members, lovers, friends, religion, faith, future goals, overall life purpose and meaning, and so forth. Those people on the dark journey have fewer adaptive beliefs, resources, and reasons for living (Bonner 2005b, 2001; Bonner & Rich, 1992, 1991, 1988a; Linehan et al., 1983), and by virtue of their dark cognitive filters tend to minimize and disqualify actual reasons for living (Ellis & Newman, 1996).

This concept in the therapeutic journey taps into a larger existential concept that was first articulated by Vincent Frankl's classic 1977 work, *Man's Search for Meaning*. The dark journey is devoid of overall life purpose and meaning so that suicide comes to be seen as a logical conclusion to a life filled with despair and hopelessness, especially in light of the belief that this is all there is and all that will be. There really are no important reasons for living to stick it out, endure the pain, and wait to see whether things will get better. So what's the point? The psychotherapist must connect with the person's meaninglessness and work to provide a relationship that has meaning for the suicidal person. In addition to the therapeutic relationship, encouraging spiritual exploration or faith development, when appropriate, can be powerfully instrumental in giving the person's life meaning in a bigger picture beyond himself or herself, and lead to a purposeful, light-filled journey. For too long, I think too many therapists have been hesitant about spiritual and religious matters as a result of their scientific training or personal struggles. When it comes to suicide, faith matters greatly, and if it leads to peace of mind, purpose in living, and goodwill toward others, it can become the power source to transform the dark journey into one of light, relief, hope, and reasons for living.

Before concluding this section on other dark suicide ideas, I would like to emphasize that the psychotherapist must be aware of the possibility of reality breaks along the dark journey. Psychoses are a significant risk factor for suicide ideation, attempts, and completions (Warman, Forman, Henriques, Brown, & Beck, 2004). Whether it is command hallucinations to suicide or delusional beliefs that glamorize suicide, the psychotherapist must get at the meaning of suicide within the person's mental world. Only the safety of a therapeutic relationship with trust and rapport can lessen a person's fear and paranoia and, some of the time, guide a person to seek relief from symptoms, such as through the use of antipsychotic medication. This can be very difficult, particularly when the suicide idea is egosyntonic for the person's journey. Sometimes it is only the depth and meaning of the therapeutic relationship that will engage a person to voluntarily try (or risk) an intervention that he or she does not necessarily believe he or she needs.

3

The Dark Emotions

In returning to Kral's (1994) summary of the suicide idea, it is viewed as an escape from unbearable psychological pain, or the dark emotions. The relation between mood disorders and suicide is strong. Salzman (1999) summarized the available research by noting that people with Major Depression have at least a 15 percent lifetime risk of suicide and represent up to 85 percent of actual suicides. Jamison (1999) summarized the research for Manic-Depression, or currently called Bipolar Disorder, and noted that suicide accounts for 20 percent of the deaths of people with this illness. He also reported that one in four people with Manic-Depressive illness will attempt suicide. Other researchers have identified the following emotions in the suicide journey: severe anxiety and agitation (Fawcett, 1999), anger and rage (Van Pragg, 2001), humiliation and self-hatred (Shneidman, 1999), and desperation (Hendin, Maltsberger, Hass, Szanto, & Rabinowicz, 2004).

The psychotherapist working with the suicidal person must understand the experience of depression along the dark journey. Unlike the relatively normal ups and downs or occasional blues of living, depression is a constant theme of the person as he or she struggles with the suicide idea. Feeling emotionally dark and cold, the depressed person interprets life events, good and bad, through the negative, self-defeating filter, reflecting helplessness, hopelessness, and worthlessness. No matter how positively the event or person might be seen by others, the depressed person only sees it as negative and reflective of self-failure. Good-intentioned efforts on the part of others to point out the good or do good for the depressed person often brings frustration and rein-

forces the self-image that something is very wrong with him or her.
The person is in the dark cave and cannot see light, good, or anything
else in terms of his or her existence.

Over time, depression leaves the person tired, or even exhausted.
Life responsibilities, work, relationships, and even basic self-care are
experienced as a burden. The person has no initiative, desire, or energy
to even try to meet these obligations. Depressed people love to sleep, as
it provides relief and escape from a burdensome, worrisome life. Ironically, many people with depression have difficulties falling or staying
asleep, which disrupts their only escape and brings more frustration
and upset. When the depression becomes too much to bear, the idea of
suicide progresses into suicide contemplation, suicide decision making
and planning, and eventual suicide action, usually when there is just
enough energy that the person can muster to carry out the suicide
action.

The addition of mania gives the depressed person a sense of euphoria with mood cycling between extreme highs and extreme lows. In
time, these mood fluctuations wear out the person, causing him or her
feel to feel more worthless and hopeless in light of the uplifting experiences, which have been short-lived and deceptive. Ultimately, when
the person finally plunges into a severe depression, the suicide idea is
rapidly fueled into action to escape intense despair.

Severe anxiety, panic, and agitation can also color the dark journey
of the suicidal mind. Feelings of restlessness, irritability, fear, and a
heightened state of psychophysiological arousal create an extremely
uncomfortable emotional state for the suicidal person. Sensations of
massive body tightening and crawling skin make the journey unbearable. Suicide becomes the only way out of this intolerable emotional
choking.

Anger and rage directed toward the self also make up part of the
dark journey. The person comes to hate himself or herself and cannot
stand living. The person believes he or she does not deserve to live and
should be punished out of self-hate and disgust. When comparing self

with others, the person feels inferior and humiliated. Suicide is the ultimate punishment—getting rid of self, mutilating self, killing self.

The dark emotions of the suicide journey for some eventually turn into psychache, mental perturbation, and consuming psychological pain (Shneidman, 2005, 2001). Each person's threshold (or tolerance level) for emotional pain is unique, and the psychotherapist must uncover what that level may be for each person. When the threshold is reached, the person's suicide idea is driven into action, sometimes as a desperate attempt to escape. The psychotherapist must validate the person's emotional pain, offer avenues of relief, and fortify and (if possible) elevate the person's controls or psychache threshold.

4

Psychache and Dark Physiology

The concept of psychache threshold is extremely theoretically compelling. It is at the heart of treating suicidality and preventing a suicide
attempt or its completion from occurring. The therapist should ask the
person how he or she would know whether the threshold is being pres-
sured. The suicidal person knows better than anyone what his or her
distress level is and how much more he or she can tolerate. Past episodes of dyscontrol, past suicide attempt lethality, and current suicide
intention are prophetic for the therapist in anticipating the suicide
journey's future. Past suicide history is the best predictor of future suicide ideas and actions (Bonner, 2001; Roy, 1992).

In terms of mental illness, both for thought and mood disorders,
there is compelling evidence that genes and biology play an important
role (Mann & Arango, 1999). These researchers also noted that several
studies have shown an independent effect of genetics and familial
transmission in suicide, beyond the link with the affective and thought
disorders. The neurotransmitter serotonin has been given considerable
attention in recent years, both in relation to affective disorders (Roy,
1992), and to the impulsiveness, inhibition, and aggression (Mann &
Arango, 1999) associated with suicide. It is very important that the
psychotherapist obtain a thorough history of the suicidal person's family history of affective disorders and suicide. The existence of a serotonin dysfunction may potentiate the risk for reaching the psychache
threshold and losing control through suicide action.

In addition to psychache physiology, the use of the dark spirits (e.g.,
alcohol and drug abuse) greatly increases the risk for symptom exacer-

bation, dyscontrol, and suicide (Weiss & Hufford, 1999). The use of substances usually starts out for medicinal purposes in changing dark emotions to positive feelings such as relaxation, calmness, or euphoria. The presence of an affective disorder in the substance abuser is quite common. In time, the use of substances often has a paradoxical effect and in fact makes the depression, anxiety, agitation, and psychache worse. The person with the suicide idea and depression on the dark journey using the dark spirits is headed for dyscontrol and suicide action. Many people who attempt suicide or kill themselves are intoxicated at the time of their acts.

Finally, in terms of psychache threshold, some people with the suicide idea who repeatedly engage in suicide attempts or self-mutilation are given the label of "borderline personalities," in my opinion sometimes for the misdirected benefit of the psychotherapist and at the expense of the person. Linehan (1999) suggests these people suffer from an unknown neurological dysfunction or disorder whereby excessive emotionality and inadequate modulation functions interact with invalidating family environments to produce chronic suicidality. The psychotherapist's role is to validate the person's emotional experience, meanwhile coaching the person to learn regulation techniques to compensate for the neurological dysfunction. Like others on the dark journey of the suicide idea, people with these characteristics are driven to suicide action to escape intolerable psychological pain. Too often, psychotherapists have misinterpreted the self-harming behavior as part of some psychoanalytic or psychodynamic drama in which the patient is "acting out" to punish the transference object or the psychotherapist. Such efforts trivialize, minimize, and invalidate the person's suicide idea, the dark journey, and unbearable psychological pain, and may ultimately contribute more to the person's psychache and hopelessness, increasing the odds of more suicide action. These people with the borderline label are not different or less suicidal than others without this label on the dark journey. Furthermore, 10 percent of these labeled individuals, according to Linehan (1999), go on to commit suicide, a rate that is similar to the suicide rates by others who suffer other mental illnesses. In addition, the suicide rate for people with this label who have self-injured or attempted suicide is twice that of those with no history of suicide actions.

The psychotherapist's role for people with this label, just as it is for other people on the dark journey, is to connect with the journey, offer acceptance and understanding of why the suicide ideas make "sense," and validate the emotional pain. Only then can the therapist gently offer avenues of relief and teach skills to help the person fortify and elevate his or her psychache threshold. According to Dr. Linehan (1987, p. 272), the key components of treatment are:

> Acknowledgment of the patient's sense of emotional desperation (validation strategies), a matter of fact attitude about current and previous parasuicidal and other dysfunctional behaviors....an active attempt to "reframe" suicidal and other dysfunctional behaviors as part of the patient's learned problem-solving repertoire, and continuing effort to focusing therapy on active problem-solving...the therapist actively teaches emotional regulation, interpersonal effectiveness, distress tolerance, and self-management skills.

5

The Dark Journey: A Developmental, Stress, and Coping Process

The dark journey of the suicidal mind is initiated by stressful life events, interpersonal losses, or problems in living. Suicide ideators, attempters, and completers have been shown to experience significantly more negative life stress than the general population or other clinical groups (Brent, Perpez, Moritz, Baugher, Roth, Balach, & Schweers, 1993; Cochrane & Robertson, 1975; Dixon, Rumford, Heppner, & Lips, 1992; Luscomb, Clum, & Patsiokas, 1980; Paykel, Pruusoff, & Myers, 1975; van der Kolk, Perry, & Herman, 1991; Yang & Clum, 1996). When a person is taxed by stress and the person's efforts to reduce stress are unsuccessful, the person is apt to develop negative appraisals of stress and coping that are self defeating, thus increasing the stress of future negative events and coping failures. Over time, these negative appraisals and coping failures lead to depression, hopelessness, and the suicide idea and its progression (Clum & Febbraro, 2004).

Several integrative models of stress and coping on the dark journey of the suicide idea have been proposed that can help guide psychotherapists in the process of therapy.

King (1988) has proposed a transactional model of suicide development. She views psychache as the final common pathway to suicide action that progresses over time from the dynamic interplay of personal vulnerabilities and negative life events. Variations in genetic and temperamental vulnerability, rearing environments, learning experiences, and interpersonal stressors are hypothesized to result in multiple pathways of coping. Factors such as mental illness, substance abuse, social isolation, and other psychosocial vulnerabilities are thought to move a person across different paths over the life span. Problems in one area may magnify other areas, while strengths, coping resources, and psychosocial protectors can minimize other areas and protect the individual from stressful life events and pro-suicide factors. Without such buffers, the suicidal person is viewed as at risk for developing and surpassing the psychache threshold and moving into suicide action.

The stress-diathesis vulnerability model posits that individuals progress on the dark journey of suicide as the result of select psychosocial vulnerabilities that interfere with effective coping and problem-solving (Bonner, 2005a, 2005b, 2001, 1992). With increased life stress, negative stress appraisals, ineffective coping, and growing frustration and emotional upset, the person on the journey develops psychache, hopelessness, and ultimate suicide intention.

Yufit and Bongar (1992) have suggested that suicide action is caused by a breakdown in psychological equilibrium, coping with life-cycle stressors, and having a decreased capacity for a positive future orientation. Psychological equilibrium, as a healthy adaption to change, is described as a function of effective coping skills predominating over one's vulnerability to stress. Negative time equilibrium is a function of fear of the future, and nostalgia for the past. Positive time equilibrium is a function of a planned future orientation and a realistic appraisal and interpretation of past events. Finally, maintaining a vital balance during critical stressful life events is a function of resiliency and buoyant coping and adaptation abilities, predominating over vulnerability and loss of time perspective.

Along similar lines, our work (Bonner, 2005a, 2005b, 2001; Bonner & Rich, 1992, 1991, 1988a, 1988b; Rich & Bonner, 1990) has described a state-of-mind model of suicide, which is hypothesized to develop in four stages: passive suicide ideation, suicide contemplation, suicide planning and decision making, and suicide action. Progression through these stages is viewed as a function of a hopeless state of mind, as the result of the person's current and past biopsychosocial coping transactions. In this dynamic process, psychache and suicide intention are thought to develop as the result of pressure on each person's unique threshold for emotional pain. These transactions are proposed to vary as the result of sex, age, race, and culture.

Considering these integrative models, several implications for psychotherapy with the suicidal person are noteworthy. First, psychotherapy is a relationship process by patient invitation and therapist acceptance to understand suicide as a process or dark journey, consisting of biopsychosocial systems of the person transacting with life stress over time. Second, these models suggest the psychotherapist must willingly, directly, and systematically join the suicidal person on this dark journey. The suicide idea and psychache of the person on the journey must be validated by the psychotherapist as making "experiential sense" in the course of his or her coping over time. Third, the psychache threshold must be collaboratively clarified by the therapist and the suicidal person, and they must work together to anticipate and prepare for possible triggers that might pressure the threshold. In addition, the therapist and suicidal person must work toward accessing and building protectors or resources that might reduce psychache and raise the threshold level. Fourth, the other dark suicide ideas (e.g., hopelessness, pro-suicide beliefs, tunnel vision, problem-solving deficits), the dark emotions (e.g., depression, anxiety, mania, rage, self-hate), and dark physiology (e.g., serotonin deficiencies, substance abuse, familial transmission, and possible neurological deficits related to excessive emotionality and regulation) must be explored in psychotherapy and integrated within the person's coping transactions over time.

Ultimately, the process of psychotherapy writes the life story for the suicidal person's dark journey. All the pieces fit together in a life story of the dark journey, which explains how the suicide idea, psychache, and suicide action have come about. Within the story, the suicide idea makes perfect experiential sense. The therapist must see it and feel it, and be able to convey to the person his or her understanding of the story and why suicide has come to make sense. In so doing, the therapist tells the person he or she is okay, worthy of love and compassion, that his or her dark journey is heartbreaking, and that he or she wants to do everything possible to reduce the pain, replace the suicide idea with a life idea, and ultimately help the suicidal person write a future life story and take a new journey where light, hope, and possibilities replace darkness.

6

Some Helpful Tools: Assessment

In working with suicidal people in psychotherapy, the therapist must first determine whether the person will benefit more from outpatient psychotherapy or from alternative or more intensive treatments. As discussed earlier, the suicide idea is the focal point in which the therapist must gather information about its current and past frequency, severity, intentions, and triggers. In addition, the therapist should determine in which stage of the suicide idea the person is—that of passive suicide ideation, suicide contemplation, suicide planning and decision making, or suicide action. In the event that the person has made a suicide attempt in the past, it will be important to determine the person's intentions before, during, and after the attempt; the lethality of the act; and whether any of these characteristics are present currently. Generally, if a person is at one of the first three stages, has not reached the psychache threshold, is not actively abusing substances, and is able to engage in a therapeutic process, then he or she should be able to benefit from outpatient psychotherapy.

Such information is primarily obtained by the clinical interview. It goes without saying that even in the beginning, the therapist must connect with the person and offer acceptance and empathy in order to obtain accurate information. If available, examining past treatment records and interviewing significant others will assist the therapist in making a thorough, objective assessment. Traditional psychological testing (Eyman & Eyman, 1992) is limited in shedding light on the suicide idea but may be useful in identifying underlying psychological processes and ego functions. However, specifically designed instruments that target the suicide idea and its components have been shown to be especially helpful in guiding the therapist in suicide assessment. Table 6–1 outlines several common instruments that assess the suicide idea.

Table 6–1 Some Common Assessment Instruments of the Dark Journey

THE DARK SUICIDE IDEA

Scale for Suicide Ideators

Beck, A.T., Kovacs, M., & Weissman, A. (1979). Assessment of suicidal ideation: The Scale for Suicide Ideators. Journal of Consulting and Clinical Psychology, 47, 343–352.

Suicide Intent Scales

Beck, A.T., Schuyler, D., & Herman, I. (1974). Development of suicide intent scales. In A.T. Beck, H.L.P. Resnick, & D.J. Lettieri (Eds.), The Prediction of Suicide (pp. 45–56). Bowie: MD: Charles Press.

Suicidal Ideation Questionnaires

Reynolds, W.M. (1987) Suicidal Ideation Questionnaires. Odessa, FL: Psychological Assessment Resources

OTHER DARK SUICIDE IDEAS

Beck Hopelessness Scale

Beck, A. T. (1987). Beck Hopelessness Scale. San Antonio, TX: The Psychological Corporation.

Problem-Solving Inventory

Heppner, P.P., & Petersen, C.H. (1982). The development and implications of a personal problem-solving inventory. Journal of Counseling Psychology, 29, 166–175.

Reasons for Living Inventory

Linehan, M. (1985). Reasons for living inventory. In P.A. Keller & L.G. Ritt (Eds.), Innovations in Clinical Practice: A Source Book (Vol. 4, pp. 321–330). Sarasota, FL: Professional Resource Exchange.

DARK EMOTIONS

The Revised Beck Depression Inventory

Beck, A.T., & Steer, R.A. (1987). Manual for the Revised Beck Depression Inventory. San Antonio, TX: The Psychological Corporation.

The Psychological Pain Assessment Scale

Shneidman, E. (1999). The psychological pain assessment scale. Suicide and Life-Threatening Behavior, 29, 287–294.

Clinical Anxiety Inventory

Beck, A. T., Epstein, N., Brown, G., & Steer, R.A. (1988). An inventory for measuring clinical anxiety: Psychometric properties. Journal of Consulting and Clinical Psychology, 56, 893–897.

The Multidimensional Anger Inventory

Siegel, J.M. (1987). The multidimensional anger inventory. In P. Keller & S. Heymen (eds.), Innovations in Clinical Practice: A Source Book (pp. 279–288). Sarasota, FL: Professional Resource Exchange.

Once the suicide idea is assessed, the therapist should move on to the presence of other dark ideas that fuel the dark journey. Hopelessness is a core theme of the suicide journey. The therapist should ask the person how he or she sees the future going. Is there light at the end of the tunnel or does it appear dark and hopeless? The greater the person's hopelessness, the greater the risk is for suicide action, which might necessitate other interventions or suicide precautions. Important questions to ask yourself as the therapist are—How strong is the therapeutic relationship? Can hope be fostered.? If the person is disengaged and unable to participate in a meaningfully therapeutic dialogue, alternative interventions will be indicated, such as a psychiatric referral, hospitalization, and so forth. Table 6–1 outlines some common measures of the other dark suicide ideas that can guide the therapist in the assessment.

Other targets for assessment include the presence of pro-suicide beliefs, reasons for living, and the suicide fantasy, as discussed earlier. The more ingrained the suicide beliefs, the fewer the reasons for living, the greater the suicide intention and wish to die in the suicide fantasy, the greater the risk is for suicide action. Basic questions to ask are: "Tell me about your suicide idea; what makes you believe it is a possible solution? What do you see as the costs and benefits of acting on your suicide idea? What has stopped you from acting on your suicide idea? Who or what keeps you going? Tell me how you picture your suicide—what will it accomplish? How will it affect others? What do you want it to accomplish? Figure 6–1 provides a "Suicide Contemplation Analysis" that has the person dissect his or her suicide idea according to situations, costs, benefits, suicide beliefs, suicide fantasies, and associated affect/emotion.

Figure 6–1 Suicide Contemplation Analysis

Date	Situation	Suicide Ideas	Costs/Benefits	Suicide Fantasy	Emotion

This tool can help the therapist and suicidal person establish a suicide idea baseline that can be reassessed again and again as therapy unfolds and interventions are implemented

Once the dark suicide ideas have been assessed, the psychotherapist will want to assess the emotional state of the person. Basic questions to ask are: Tell me how you feel; how long have you felt this way? How do these feelings influence your life? How is your sleep? How is your appetite? Are you able to attend to and concentrate on daily tasks? What about your energy level? Do you seem to always feel this way, or do you have periods where your feelings change, if so, to what do they change? The Suicide Contemplation Analysis also taps the associated emotions with the suicide idea and can establish common emotional patterns or themes for the person's suicide journey. The therapist also needs to attend to the person's presentation in the interview. What is the presenting affect? What is the speech content? How does it flow? What is the body posture? How is the eye contact? The therapist in assessment is on a search for some of the common emotions of the dark journey, as outlined in Chapter 3. This search comprises depression, mania, anxiety, agitation, rage, and self-hate. Table 6–1 also outlines some common measures of mood to help guide the therapist in this process. In the likely event that the person is suffering from a mood disorder, the psychotherapist, if not a psychiatrist, should consider making a psychiatric referral for a medication regimen to help reduce symptoms. The assessment and such a referral will only be as successful as the quality of the therapeutic relationship.

Perhaps most critical in suicide risk assessment is the notion of psychache threshold. Has the person reached or is the person close to reaching the breaking point where he or she cannot tolerate any more emotional pain? It is at the press of this subjective point that suicide action becomes imminent, most especially if the method is at hand. Only a trust-based therapeutic relationship can establish what the unique threshold level is for a given individual. If the person is suffering from a psychotic illness and/or is abusing alcohol or drugs, it should be assumed that the threshold has been or will be met, as controls will inevitably break down. Prompt detoxification procedures, crisis intervention services, or psychiatric hospitalization will be needed to stabilize the person before he or she can resume psychotherapy.

There are several other considerations in determining psychache threshold for the suicidal person. First, the therapist will want to inquire about past episodes of dyscontrol, past suicide attempt lethality, and current suicide intention. Second, the therapist will want to ask about any family history of mental illness, affective disorder, and suicide. Third, the therapist will want to assess indirect evidence genetically, historically, and currently for a serotonin deficiency. Finally, does the person's dark journey involve excessive emotionality and poor regulation, suggesting a possible underlying neurological dysfunction?

Figure 6–2 provides a "Self-Analysis of Mood Controls" to help the suicidal person and therapist determine the level of controls and ability to tolerate emotional pain. If the person has not reached the threshold, psychotherapy can proceed as usual, with one exception. The issue of possible future psychache dyscontrol must be identified, anticipated, projected, and prepared for.

Figure 6–2 Self-Analysis of Mood Controls

What are the reasons you have not acted on your suicide decision and plan?

_____   _____
_____   _____
_____   _____

What would it take for you to act on your decision and plan?

_____
_____

How likely is that? _____

How likely is it that you will attempt suicide today? _____

tomorrow? _____

in a few days? _____

in a week? _____

in two weeks? _____

in a month? _____

**In terms of your depression and emotional pain, will you be able to tolerate it
today?** _____

tomorrow? _____

in a few days? _____

in a week? _____

in two weeks? _____

in a month? _____

How much more can you take before you lose control? _____
_____
_____

What might happen or what emotion might get worse that would push a person to the breaking point? And, if that happened, what would the person do or what better alternative can the person do? It is at this point that a "Pro-Living Relationship Agreement" can be fortified, with a viable escape or safety net should the threshold be pressed (See Figure 6–3).

<u>Figure 6–3 Pro-Living Relationship Agreement</u>

Because of our work together, I _____, realize that you care about me and don't want to see anything happen that would harm me. Because I care about you and our relationship, I promise that I will do everything that I can to not act on my suicide decision and plan and will do my best to focus on living, and not dying. You have my word that if I start to feel worse or think I am going to lose control, I will immediately try to reach you at _____. If I cannot reach you immediately, I promise that I will call the ambulance at _____ or call my family at _____ and request that I be taken to the hospital. I also realize from our work together that I care about

_____

_____, and would want to do my best to avoid hurting them by acting on my suicide plan.

Agreed Upon By: _____

                        Client   **Date**

                        _____

                        Therapist   **Date**

Unlike the controversial "no suicide contracts," this agreement is a relationship agreement reflecting a closeness, trust, and care for emotional pain and the possible loss of control. It emphasizes the person's reasons for living, including the therapeutic relationship, and also provides a plan of safety should the person feel he or she was going to lose control. The therapeutic relationship is the life saver, not any form of a written contract.

In summarizing the assessment of these components of the dark journey, the therapist may feel overwhelmed in terms of the various data points. As discussed in Chapter 5, suicide is best understood as a developmental, biopsychosocial process as a person copes with stress over time. In this spirit, Arnold Lazarus (1995) developed multimodal assessment as an organizing guide and integrative system for the clinician. Specifically, he proposed that clinical problems can be assessed and treated by targeting the **B.A.S.I.C. I.D.** modality systems of human functioning. For our purposes, we (Bonner & Michalik-Bonner, 1996) applied this scheme to suicidality, which is viewed as a biopsychosocial process that is defined, determined, and maintained by some transaction of **Behavior, Affect, Sensations, Images, Cognitions, Interpersonal Systems,** and **Drugs** (genetics/physiology/substance abuse). The culmination of these system transactions over time is hypothesized to lead to ineffective coping and problem solving, varying levels of hopelessness, psychache, and ultimate suicide intention. Table 6–2 outlines a multimodal assessment of suicidality and can easily guide the therapist in evaluation and treatment.

Table 6–2 Multimodal Assessment of BASIC ID Targets of Suicidality

(Bonner & Michalik-Bonner, 1996)

BEHAVIOR—Past suicide attempts (intention, lethality, motives, life/death wishes, opportunities for rescue; etc.)
—Current planning behaviors (acquiring a method, obtaining intoxicants, suicide/good-bye communications, preparing a will, giving away possessions, writing a suicide note, etc.)
—History of circumstances of behavioral dyscontrol and coping breakdown
—Family behavioral history of suicidality

AFFECT—Depression
—Mania
—Self-Hate
—Panic/Anxiety/Agitation
—Perturbation and Psychache

SENSATIONS—Tension/psychophysiological arousal and agitation
—Hallucinations/delusions with suicide or death themes
—Fatigue, withdrawal, psychomotor retardation

IMAGES—Suicide/death fantasies
—Helpless/hopeless images

COGNITIONS—Suicide ideation and contemplation
—Cognitive rigidity and tunnel vision
—Hopeless expectancies
—Lack of adaptive, life-oriented beliefs
—Psychotic processing, weak cognitive controls

INTERPERSONAL—Social isolation
SYSTEMS—Negative life stress
—Taxing sociodemographic/cultural influences

DRUGS—Biochemistry of affective and thought disorders
—Genetic influences
—Alcohol and drug use/abuse

**Note: The foregoing is from "The Suicidal Patient in Private Practice: A Multimodal Approach" (p.5) by R.L. Bonner and D.R. Michalik-Bonner, 1996, Psychotherapy in Private Practice, 14(4), 1–15. Copyright by the Haworth Press. Reprinted with permission.

7

Some Helpful Tools:
Interventions

By now, the reader should be clear that the position of this work is that the psychotherapy relationship is the heart and soul of changing the direction of the dark journey. Unconditional regard, compassion, and validation of the suicidal person's journey fosters meaning, hope, and reasons for living in the midst of life problems, emotional pain, and despair. Moreover, the relationship influences the suicidal person to consider alternatives, try new behaviors, and develop new coping and problem-solving skills. The idea of the therapist as a "coach" on the suicidal person's team to use "collaborative empiricism" in testing and modifying the suicide ideas and its dark components is invaluable (Weishaar & Beck, 1990).

In terms of coaching and the actual psychotherapy, cognitive interventions for the suicidal person have been given the most attention in recent years, due to the core cognitive component of the suicide idea and its progression. This component comprises suicide ideas, contemplation, planning, suicide beliefs, problem-solving deficits, hopeless expectations, reasons for living, and suicide fantasies. Beginning with the suicide idea, the therapist should help the person identify the trigger and escape function of the idea. Most people who experience passive suicide thoughts in reaction to some life stress or problem of living only do so passively. Once the trigger is identified, therapeutic efforts should be made to resolve the problem or stressor.

For the person whose suicide idea is more elaborate and contempla-
tive, the therapist should assist the person in conducting a rational, evidence-based cost-benefit analysis of the suicide idea. It should be
expected that the suicidal person, as the result of negative cognitive filters, will initially tend to magnify the benefits and minimize the costs.
The therapist's role will be to provide an empirically based, objective
analysis of the benefits and costs of suicide for the person and his or her
significant others. Homework assignments, writing up the analysis,
and practicing objective cost-benefit analysis will help strengthen the
person's rational thinking skills.

At the cognitive core of suicide contemplation is the presence of
pro-suicide beliefs. These beliefs must be identified, labeled, and
empirically examined in terms of reality, evidence, and probable suicide outcome. Table 7–1 outlines ten common suicide beliefs, which
therapy dialogue should uncover and systematically examine for their
evidence. Homework assignments, monitoring, and *in vivo* practice
will help develop rational beliefs in place of the suicide beliefs, and
become part of the person's coping repertoire.

Table 7–1 Common Pro-Suicide Beliefs and Their Refutation

Pro-Suicide Beliefs	Refutation
Others will be better off without me.	What is the evidence? Most people suffer trauma when someone they know or love commits suicide. Don't they at least deserve input into your decision, since it is you who says they will be better?
I can't take any more of the pain.	How much pain have you taken so far? In the past, has the pain ever gotten better? What are the chances your current pain will get better? What have you done to feel better? What else can we try?
The future is only going to get worse.	How do you know that? Can you see into the future? How many times have you felt bad and thought things wouldn't get better and then they did?
Without him/her, I've got nothing to live for.	What do you mean? Your whole life and self-worth were based on this one person? What did you have to live for before you met this person? Who else is in your life? Don't they matter to you? You mean to say there is nothing else to you but this person? What about your faith/your work/ your future goals?
I am too much of a burden to my family.	How do you know that? Have they told you the burden would be less if you were dead? Most of the time in my experience, the burden of suicide is much worse on children and family members. Don't they have the right to be involved in your decision?
At least I'll be out of here when I die.	In actuality, you will probably not be anywhere, you won't exist. Do you have any beliefs about a life hereafter? If so, where might you go? Maybe it will be worse. There are no guarantees, you know.
Nobody really cares whether I'm dead or alive.	How do you know that? Have you interviewed everyone you know? What about your loved ones? Shouldn't they have a say in this judgment, especially since they will have to live with your suicide? What about me? I care deeply about you and your life. It seems you don't care about my feelings, since I'm going to have to suffer and live with your loss. And how am I going to feel when I have to try to comfort your family.
Killing myself will show others how I felt!	How do you know that? They might disregard your suicide or simply say they always knew something was wrong with you, maybe you were crazy. Most of the time, if people didn't care about how you felt when you were alive, they *really* won't care about how you felt when you are dead. By the way, I care deeply about how you feel and want to do whatever I can to help you feel better
Death will bring me peace and no more problems.	How do you know this? Have you been dead before? Do you know of anyone who has? Have they confirmed that you will be at peace, with no more problems? What about those of us who care about you? Your death won't bring us peace, but more pain and problems. That doesn't seem fair.
It's my life and I can kill myself if I want to.	You are very right about that. You have the ultimate control and choice to live or die. I just don't believe you will really want to die once we work together and figure out how to help your problems and make you feel better. Shouldn't you at least give it a chance?

Another cognitive factor associated with the suicide idea and dark journey is a lack of effective problem-solving skills. The place to start is to identify the initial stress trigger that activated the suicide idea and its progression. What problem has come about to make the person consider suicide as a solution? As noted previously, negative life events and problem of living play an important role in initiating the suicide process. At this point, standard problem-solving training is useful, to include: a) problem definition and formulation, b) generation of alternative solutions, c) decision making, and d) implementation and verification (D'Zurilla, Nezu, & Maydeu-Oliveras, 2004). According to Clum and Febbraro (2004, p. 76):

> Treatments based on this approach are aimed at helping
> individuals (a) link unresolved problems to suicidal thoughts,
> impulses and actions; (b) increase the motivation to
> view such problems as issues to be resolved and
> managed effectively; and (c) use problem-solving
> skills to solve these problems.

The suicide fantasy is another important area for cognitive intervention. It is often helpful to have the suicidal person write out in detail his or her fantasy with regard to suicide. Questions and statements to get at this process are as follows: Tell me in your fantasy what your suicide will do—for you, others, your family, and the world. Tell me who will find you after you commit suicide and what their reaction will be. What will people who know you say about you when they learn you have committed suicide? How will your viewing and funeral go—who will come, how will they feel, what will they say? What will happen to these people as time goes on after your death? Do you have any thoughts or beliefs about what will happen to you? Is there another life for you after this? What does your faith or beliefs tell you?"

Now, once the therapist and suicidal person have a vivid picture of the suicide fantasy, the therapeutic question becomes, "Is this fantasy what you really want to happen?" If not, the benefits and rationality of the suicide idea will need to be reexamined. However, if the suicide fantasy is desired, the therapist will need to use systematic questioning through what ifs. What about other possibilities? The therapist ought to encourage patients to consider what might occur as the result of their suicide that is not part of their fantasy, as well as not desired. The therapist will then need to ask the person whether it is worth the risk to commit suicide given these possibilities. Most of the time, the person will decide it is not worth the risk after careful, rational examination.

In addition to the suicide fantasy analysis, the therapist must help the person identify his or her specific hopeless expectations according to specific situations and specific feelings. Equally important, the therapist will want to ascertain whether there are other areas or people in the person's life that do not appear hopeless. These areas should be focused on, supported, and built upon. For hopeless expectations, the therapist should coach the person to examine these empirically in terms of what has happened in the past, what has happened to others in similar situations, and what other possibilities might happen. In this process the person's expectations need to be examined in terms of the negative cognitive filter, to include problem overestimation and resource underestimation. Again, as with other skill-building methods, encouraging the person to monitor expectations over time, across situations, and across emotions will help identify what areas might need targeted to decrease hopeless expectations. Most importantly, the therapist must be mindful that his or her therapeutic relationship with the suicidal person may be all that is available for hope and meaning in the person's life.

Finally, the suicidal person's available reasons for living must be tapped, supported, and fortified. The tendency of the suicidal person to negate or minimize actual available reasons for living must be considered. Standard cognitive restructuring and rational behavior therapy can be useful in helping the person to realistically appraise his or her reasons for living and build from there. Involving family members and significant others in the therapy process may provide a reality check for the suicidal person and he or she may realize that he or she is in fact an important reason for living for significant others, which might in turn become a reason for living for the suicidal person. Again, the therapeutic relationship may become the sole reason for living for the suicidal person, emphasizing the importance for the therapist to be available, connect, and validate the dark journey of the suicidal mind. Finally, as noted before, accessing avenues other than traditional therapy should be examined and fully supported to build hope and life meaning, such as that which is often found in faith and spiritual development. William James, America's foremost psychologist and philosopher, for example, noted that faith is often the only thing that makes life worth living. As Shneidman (2004) so powerfully points out in his recent *Autopsy of a Suicidal Mind,* our relationship work must strive in every regard to demonstrate that the "unbearable" pain really can be "barely bearable" and "somehow tolerable."

In terms of resources for the therapist in implementing cognitive interventions, several works exist that are invaluable. For bibliotherapy, Paul Quinnett's (1997) *Suicide: The Forever Decision* speaks directly to the person with the suicide idea and its contemplation. He captures the eye and mind of the suicide contemplator and understands why suicide has come to make sense for the person. Dr. Quinnett then challenges the contemplator to think through the consequences if he or she was to suicide, such as the impact on family, friends, and children. He also takes a rational, evidence-based approach to helping the reader determine whether suicide actually would solve his or her problem, and whether the suicide fantasy is likely to be fulfilled with the contemplator's actual suicide. Finally, he offers alternative thinking and experimentation with new behaviors to assess the impact on the problem and the suicide idea. The reader is left with a convincing feeling that Dr. Quinnett deeply understands his or her reasons for contemplating suicide, but genuinely believes rational thinking, problem-solving skills, and accessing psychosocial supports will—most of the time—result in the contemplator deciding his or her reasons for living outweigh reasons for dying.

Another very helpful book for the suicide contemplator is called "Choosing to Live: How to Defeat Suicide Through Cognitive Therapy," written by Thomas Ellis and Cory Newman (1996). This book teaches the suicidal person a step by step therapy program to reverse the suicide process. Specific therapeutic strategies are taught to the reader to modify cognitive distortions, irrational beliefs, pro-suicide beliefs, and suicide fantasies. In addition, this book provides the suicidal person a number of skill-building exercises to reverse the suicide idea and facilitate effective, life-oriented coping.

One of the best state of the art treatment manuals for therapists working with suicidal people is called *Treating Suicidal Behavior: An Effective, Time-Limited Approach*, written by David Rudd, Thomas Joiner, and Hajan Rahab (2001). This impressive work outlines stage-specific cognitive treatment strategies in a session by session format to systematically modify the dark suicide ideas. It is invaluable in helping the therapist working with the suicidal person to develop treatment plans, session-by-session interventions, treatment-outcome assessment, and risk management.

In addition to cognitive interventions, which might also in fact reduce emotional suffering, the therapist will need to determine what other interventions may be needed to reduce psychache and the other dark emotions. Marsha Linehan's *Dialectical Behavior Therapy* is at the forefront of specific interventions to reduce and regulate emotional distress of suicidality (see Chapter 4). The efficacy of standard cognitive-behavioral interventions for mood disorders is well established (Barlow, 2004), and will not be elaborated upon here. It suffices to say that the therapist should have a good understanding of these interventions for relieving the emotional suffering and psychache associated with the suicide idea and its progression.

In addition to psychotherapy interventions, the therapist, if not a psychiatrist, should refer and support (when appropriate) the use of

antidepressant, antianxiety, and mood stabilizing medications to provide symptom relief and improve impulse control (Medina, 1998; Roy,
2001; Salzman, 1999). There is growing evidence to support the use of
selective serotonin reuptake inhibitors (SSRIs) for some people in the
treatment of depression and suicidality. First, these medications seem
to correct the serotonin deficiency associated with depression and anxiety and provide significant relief. Second, these medications again
improve the serotonin levels that, when low, are associated with poor
affect tolerance, dysregulation, and aggression, which are in turn linked
with suicide (Van Praag, 2001). Third, these medications have less
bothersome side effects and are safer than traditional tricyclic antidepressants that have the potential for fatal overdose (Salzman, 1999).
However, each person is different and the decision—to use, not use, or
what to use—about medication is a clinical, medical decision. It is the
position of this work that the decision to use any psychotropic medication with suicidal people should be made by a board-certified psychiatrist who has specialized training in the treatment of suicidality. It
cannot be overemphasized with suicidal people that all medications
need to be closely monitored, especially with individuals who have progressed to the suicide preparation stage and who are not well-regulated
emotionally. Recently, there has been some attention given to the possibility that some medications may increase suicide risk for certain people, therefore requiring careful examination and ongoing monitoring
by the prescribing psychiatrist. Finally, for some people with high suicide intent, previous lethal suicide attempts, or who have serious affective or thought disorders that are resistant to medication, consideration
for the use of electroconvulsive therapy (ECT) should be made (Guttmacher, 1994; Salzman, 1999). This treatment can be dramatically
effective in improving mood and lowering suicidality for individuals
who have not been helped by other therapeutic or medicative means.

Applying the multimodal model to interventions for specific stages
of the suicide process, Figure 7–1 outlines stage specific interventions
based on the possible saliency of particular **B.A.S.I.C. I.D.** modalities.

This is a theoretical attempt to integrate therapeutic strategies, suicide stages, and suicide modalities into a practical guide for the psychotherapist. It should simply be used as a guide that is modified and tailored according to the unique clinical **B.A.S.I.C. I.D.** picture of each person on the dark journey of the suicide idea.

Figure 7-1 Stage Specific Multimodal Interventions for the Suicidal Person

Stage 4 Suicide Action-B.A.S.I.C. I.D. Interventions
- Emergency medical care
- Suicide precautions/psychiatric hospitalization
- Intensify mental health, social, and psychiatric interventions via comprehensive **B.A.S.I.C. I.D.** multimodal assessment and treatment plan
- If no improvement, consider ECT

Stage 3 Suicide Planning and Decision-Making-A/S/D Interventions
- Reduce negative affect/sensations via cognitive-behavioral and pharmacological interventions
- Improve mood modulation and affect tolerance via dialectical behavior therapy, mood stabilizing medications, and/or SSRI antidepressants
- Detoxification if abusing substances
- Target environmental conditions, including removal of method, implementing safety net
- If psychache threshold intact, enter into Pro-Living Relationship Agreement with safety net (e.g., emergency on-call, family call, staying with family/friends, ambulance call)
- If psychache threshold pressed, consider crisis stabilization/hospitalization services

Stage 2 Suicide Contemplation-I/C Interventions
- Examine suicide ideas, costs/benefits, intentions, wishes to live/die
- Use cognitive therapy to challenge, disrupt, and replace pro-suicide beliefs, suicide fantasies, helpless/hopeless images, negative future expectations
- Access and build reasons for living
- Teach problem-solving skills

Stage 1 Passive Suicide Ideation-I 2 Interventions
- Access/increase family and social supports
- Identify/resolve psychosocial problem trigger

Psychache Threshold --------------

A V O P E L E S S N E S

S B-ehavior, A-ffect, S-ensations, I-mages, C-ognitions, I-2-nterpersonal Systems, D-rugs (Physiology/Substance Abuse)

8

Case Vignettes of the Dark Journey

Case 1: "Thomas" (Stage 1 Passive Suicide Ideation)

Thomas called my office at the suggestion of his pastor. He was a thirty-three-year-old male, married with two daughters, ages six and nine. Thomas reported that he had just been fired from his job of ten years as a mid-level manager in the food service industry. The company claimed that he had miscalculated sales funds on several occasions. The company had a pattern of letting go of managers that had been with the company for more than eight years.

Thomas arrived at my office well-groomed but obviously anxious. When asked what brought him in, Thomas indicated he had been fired from his job of ten years and felt betrayed by his company to which he had given much of his life. Thomas maintained that he was innocent of the charge and could not believe that his company would make up such an accusation to get rid of him. Thomas expressed feelings of embarrassment in having to tell his family, friends, and neighbors that he had lost his job. He also reported feeling like he had let his family down and had no idea how he was going to provide a living for his family. In this discussion, Thomas made a statement that "they probably would be better off without me." At that point, I told Thomas that I could understand how he felt and wanted to find out how I could best help him. I then told him that I was unsure what he meant by the comment that his family would be better off without him. Thomas' eyes teared up and he disclosed that he felt he was a failure as a father and husband. I asked Thomas whether he was having thoughts of killing himself. He hesitantly responded, "not really...maybe just for a minute." He went on to say, "I could never do that; my kids need me. I'll find some work to do and we've got some money saved to get us through. Our families are in the area and will help."

Thomas did not have a mental health treatment history, did not abuse substances, and denied ever contemplating suicide or making an attempt before. His family was without a history of mental illness, depression, or suicide. This was Thomas's first time seeing a psychotherapist at the urging of his pastor. He came from a traditional, religious family with a rather domineering mother who was quite skilled at making her children feel guilty for anything less than perfect behavior. His father was quiet, easy-going, and chose not to rock the boat when it came to family matters or disagreement with his wife.

Multimodal Stage Analysis and Interventions

Thomas is having brief, fleeting thoughts of suicide in reaction to the stress of a job loss. He is at Stage 1 of the suicide process. His emotional upset is directly related to the **Interpersonal Systems Modality (I2)** of the stress associated with being fired from his job. In addition, as a secondary focus, Thomas seems to hold some unrealistic beliefs about success, failure, responsibility, and guilt, initiated from his childhood rearing (**Cognitions Modality-C**).

Psychotherapy will primarily target the stressor or problem of job loss (**I2**). Thomas' feelings of upset will be validated and his brief, fleeting thoughts of suicide will be connected as having escape value. All of Thomas's reasons for living will be reinforced. Therapy then will need to help Thomas with the problem at hand, namely, what is he going to do about this job loss. Possible problem-solving steps will include hiring an attorney to advocate on his behalf, making contact with colleagues at other companies that might be able to assist him with another job, completing job applications, preparing for job interviews (including what he is going to say when asked about his previous employment), and so forth. While not necessary for this case, if Thomas wishes to pursue his emotional reaction in greater depth, standard cognitive **(C)** methods to challenge, dispute, and replace some of his underlying beliefs about success and responsibility will be useful.

Case 2: "Allison" (Stage 2 of Suicide Contemplation)

Allison called my office at the suggestion of her friend, who had seen me years ago for marital therapy. Allison was a forty-one-year-old female who had recently discovered that her husband of nineteen years was involved in a gay relationship. Her husband initiated this disclosure, apologized for his unfaithfulness, but told her he wanted a divorce and needed to live out this relationship.

Allison arrived at my office downcast, with poor eye contact and limited speech. She did not initiate conversation. When asked what was going on, Allison broke down in tears. I responded that I could tell she was in a lot of pain and she should take her time telling me what had caused her pain. With some hesitation, Allison began her story. She indicated that she knew something was wrong with her marriage from the beginning, "I felt empty…. Something was not right. He was always distant." She went on to say that, as far back as she could remember, the relationship lacked closeness, and sexual intimacy was nonexistent. Allison described her husband as being a workaholic who was seldom home, and when he was home he was always working on some project. Allison disclosed that her life was "very lonely" and that she believed the problem was with her. Allison shared that she had always felt like the problem, and felt "wrong" and "bad." Allison revealed that she came from an alcoholic family. Her father was frequently intoxicated and would physically abuse her and her mother, often calling them whores. Allison ran away from home at age sixteen and got involved in an abusive relationship. Eventually she got out of that relationship by getting involved with her current husband. This relationship was not physically abusive, but was described as unemotional, lacking affection, and more of a business arrangement. Her husband took care of her financially and she took care of the domestic responsibilities. Allison remembered always feeling like something was wrong with her and that she was "unlovable," as reinforced by her husband's dearth of emotional involvement coupled with her past abusive relationships.

Allison indicated that she was seriously thinking about suicide without a plan. She could not see herself making it on her own, and she did not believe she deserved or could find someone that would love her. Allison expressed feelings of worthlessness and despair, believing suicide would end her emotional suffering. She had never been in mental health treatment before but admitted that, when she was a teenager, she would severely abuse alcohol, and on two occasions cut her wrist when she was in her bedroom and would hear her father cursing and beating her mother. Allison denied abusing substances or making any suicide attempts over the past five years. The family history was positive for alcoholism and depression, but negative for suicide.

Multimodal Analysis and Interventions

Allison is at Stage 2 of suicide contemplation. She is seriously thinking about suicide and believes it would provide a number of benefits to her current bleak existence. Her suicide idea is primarily related to the **Cognitions/Images Modality (C/I)**, holding beliefs that she is worthless, unlovable, undeserving of good, and with a future of only the same or worse. She also ascribes to other pro-suicide beliefs, such as that she will be better off dead, she deserves to be dead, and all her problems and pain will go away with suicide. Therapy would use cognitive therapy to identify these pro-suicide beliefs and negative expectations **(C/I)** and work toward an evidence-based, objective analysis of these ideas and seek to refute, disrupt, and replace them with realistic appraisals of self, external events, and significant others. In addition, the therapist will try to identify any existing reasons for living and use these in the cost-benefit analysis of the suicide idea. Allison is obviously depressed, and if these cognitive suicide contemplation interventions do not improve her mood, the **Affect Modality** (**A**) should be targeted by using standard cognitive-therapy methods for depression, as well as a possible referral for psychiatric medication (**Drugs-Physiology/Substance Abuse Modality** (**D**)). Once her thinking and mood improve and suicide is no longer being contemplated, therapy may address the **Interpersonal Systems Modality** (**I2**), which has to do with coping with a divorce, finding a job to support herself, and developing assertiveness skills to acquire healthy, supportive relationships.

Most importantly, the psychotherapeutic relationship is the power source for Allison to feel understood, validated, and willing to risk trying new behaviors and new ways of thinking. Ultimately, it will be this relationship that shows Allison that she is worthy, lovable, and deserving of much better than life has given her so far. The psychotherapist will become the beacon of light to her, to see possibilities and hope beyond the dark journey, that she is worthy of a life and future of good things and that she has in fact the skills and confidence to work toward positive goal obtainment.

Case 3 "Margaret" (Stage 3 of Suicide Planning and Decision Making)

Margaret is a twenty-six-year-old female who was brought to my office by her mother. Her mother reported that Margaret had just returned home with her two-year-old son after leaving her husband of three years, who had become abusive toward her son. Margaret came home very depressed and had been staying in bed, sleeping all day, and barely eating. Her mother revealed that when she was doing laundry and emptied out the pockets of a pair of Margaret's pants, she had found a letter written by Margaret to her apologizing for having to kill herself, feeling like she couldn't take it anymore, and asking her to take good care of her grandson.

Margaret was then interviewed alone. She presented as very depressed, with poor eye contact and lethargy. When asked about suicide, Margaret admitted she had been seriously thinking about suicide for some time since her husband "changed…after I became pregnant."

Apparently her husband was in medical school and was very angry that he had impregnated her. According to Margaret, he said things like, "You're trying to ruin my career! I told you no kids! You did this on purpose!" Margaret reported that she obtained a large number of narcotics in her capacity as a nurse and planned to overdose when she was living with him.

However, before she could do this, she found her two-year-old son bruised and bleeding, sobbing in his bedroom. An ambulance was called, the child was taken to the hospital, and the attending physician found several bone fractures and determined that it was physical abuse, likely at the hands of her husband. An investigation by Children and Youth Services confirmed this suspicion, and a warrant was issued for his arrest.

It was at this point that Margaret took her son and drove across several states to go back to her mother's home. Margaret indicated that she blamed herself for ruining the marriage and leaving her son alone with her husband when she knew "he hates him." She said she could not stand to live with herself and planned to go into the garage and turn the car on while everyone was asleep the night she arrived at her mother's . The only reason she did not go through with this was that she passed out from taking several sleeping pills. Her mother woke her up the next day after she found the suicide note.

Margaret came from a traditional, very religious family. She was an A student and was highly involved in church activities. She entered college and completed her nursing studies in three years. She went into nursing to help people and live out her faith's beliefs. She met her husband while doing a hospital internship where he was a first-year medical student. She quickly fell in love with him and dreamed of having a large family.

Margaret had received counseling for depression as a teenager after her father's sudden death. She has never made a suicide attempt before and has never abused alcohol or drugs. Her family history was positive for depression on her mother's side. There was no family history of suicide.

Multimodal Analysis and Interventions

Margaret is very depressed and has made the decision to suicide by carbon monoxide poisoning. She is lethargic, sleeps most of the time, and does not eat. She has been depressed before and there is a family history of depression. She has said in her writing that she "cannot take it anymore." The modalities of **Drugs (Physiology-D)**, **Affect (A)**, and **Sensations (S)** are primary intervention targets in this case. First, the level of psychache needs to be validated and understood by the therapist with the goal of determining whether the threshold can be raised and the emotional suffering decreased. Consideration for the use of SSRI antidepressant medication should be made to reduce depressive symptoms and increase controls. Establishing a safety net for Margaret until her mood improves is critical. While hospitalization might be considered, she may be able to be treated on an outpatient basis if she can engage with the therapist in a pro-living relationship agreement. Having a close relationship and living with her mother strengthens the safety net, because her mother can monitor the household, contact me if needed, drive her to the emergency room if needed, and closely supervise her daughter's intake of medications.

Once Margaret's depression and psychache are reduced and she is able to concentrate and engage in therapeutic dialogue, the next modality intervention would involve **Cognitions (C)**.

Margaret has a number of pro-suicide ideas, negative self-appraisals, and an unlikely suicide fantasy. On the positive side, her son and mother are obviously very important to her and would be considerable reasons for living. The suicide fantasy should be analyzed and taken to realistic possibilities, including the trauma and survivor guilt likely to occur in her son and mother. The images can be directed into the future with her son growing up, having a family of his own, and so forth, and the ways in which Margaret's suicide would significantly affect these outcomes. In addition, thoughts of being responsible for her husband's abusive behavior, breaking up the family, and the injuries her son sustained all need to be examined empirically and modified accordingly. Also, other reasons for living eventually will need to be explored, like her faith, her medical profession, and friends.

Once Margaret's depression and psychache lift, she works on developing more evidence-based beliefs and appraisals, and after the suicide idea is diminished, therapy will need to help Margaret deal with the triggering problems (**Interpersonal Systems-I2**). Namely, she will likely need to pursue filing for divorce, obtaining sole legal custody of her son, and possibly testifying against her ex-husband for his pending charges. In addition, Margaret will need to focus on her son: planning when and how to tell him about his father, and when age appropriate getting him involved in counseling to address his victimization. Margaret will also have to focus on her relocation, staying with her mother, and getting a job in the area.

The heart and soul underlying these interventions is an accepting and validating relationship with the therapist, in which Margaret feels safe to talk about her dark journey. The emotional anguish in Margaret is paralyzing. The therapist must be able to feel her pain and see through her eyes why suicide seems like the only way out of overwhelming darkness and despair.

The therapeutic connection provides a new and healing experience for Margaret, radically different than that to which she has been exposed. The connection, coupled with distress relief and alternative thinking, break the paralysis and open Margaret's vision to one of living—for her son, her mother, her values, and herself.

Case 4: "Joseph" (Stage 4 of Suicide Action)

Joseph was referred to my office from the social worker at an inpatient psychiatric unit of our community hospital. Joseph was being discharged after completing treatment following a suicide attempt by overdose of tranquilizers and alcohol. He was a forty-five-year-old divorced male with a long history of alcoholism, depression, and multiple suicide attempts (wrist cutting and overdoses). Joseph was being discharged on Prozac and Remeron, and would be followed up in outpatient treatment by his hospital psychiatrist.

Before evaluating Joseph for psychotherapy, I requested copies of all of his mental health records from the hospital, as well as a phone consultation with the treating psychiatrist and referring social worker. From this review, it became clear that all of Joseph's suicide attempts occurred after he had been drinking to the point of intoxication. The most recent suicide attempt was described as having been planned several days before including accumulation of a number of tranquilizers and two bottles of whiskey. The actual attempt by overdose should be considered highly lethal. Joseph described his intention to die "to get out of this misery." Fortunately, contrary to Joseph's planning, a neighbor came to his door the night of the overdose, entered his apartment after not getting a response, and called an ambulance. The neighbor, who periodically walked Joseph's dog for him, had stopped that night to take the dog for a walk.

Consultation with the treating psychiatrist revealed that Joseph had always had a good response to medication when he was not drinking. He had completed several rehabs and would frequently attend AA, but would relapse when his depression worsened, usually after stopping his medication. The psychiatrist indicated that he felt Joseph would be a good candidate for psychotherapy if sober and compliant with his prescribed medication. The psychiatrist and I agreed that the treatment contract would require Joseph to see both clinicians, remain on his medication, and remain sober. In the event that he was noncompliant, the psychiatrist agreed with me that Joseph would be evaluated immediately for voluntary—or involuntary, if necessary—psychiatric hospitalization.

Joseph came to his first appointment clear, alert, and in an unremarkable mood. He denied any current depressive symptoms, reported that he was compliant with his medication, and said he was attending

AA daily. Joseph was encouraged to talk about his life story, which involved the dark journey and suicide idea since adolescence. He came from an alcoholic family, in which his father was always intoxicated or passed out as far back as he could remember. His paternal grandfather was also an alcoholic and hospitalized twice for depression. He shot himself to death. Joseph described himself as a loner, having had only one intimate relationship, which resulted in a one year marriage that broke up due to his drinking. Joseph had no close friends and worked a number of construction jobs for brief periods of time. He was now getting income for a mental disability. Joseph denied having any reasons for living and said his only chance for a future would be if he remained sober and on his medication.

In discussing his recent suicide attempt, he revealed that he had been saved by his neighbor, someone who he would talk to "briefly" and who sometimes would "walk my dog [because] I couldn't." When asked about his dog, Joseph's facial expression brightened, he smiled and responded, "My dog's name is Bandit." He went on to say, "She's my only friend. [She's] stayed with me through all the rough times now over five years."

Multimodal Analysis and Intervention

Joseph was recently at Stage 4 of suicide action, a stage that he had been at several times before. He has a long history of the dark journey, suffered major depression and alcoholism, and came from a high-risk family for suicide. He was recently stabilized after psychiatric hospitalization, is now medication compliant, and is alcohol free. Psychotherapy would obviously reinforce medication compliance and sobriety through AA (**Drugs/Sensations/Affect Modalities**). In addition, the use of dialectical behavior therapy may prove useful for improving affect tolerance and control. A comprehensive **B.A.S.I.C. I.D.** assessment would be conducted to increase and intensify interventions across these major systems. The **Behavioral Modality** would be important in terms of clarifying his repertoire of suicidal behaviors, triggers, planning, intentions, and so forth, and developing alternative behaviors for the future. Obviously medication compliance and sobriety would also be important in modifying these suicidal behaviors. The **Cognitions/Images** modality would later become important in therapy to modify hopeless expectations and helpless images and teach effective problem-solving skills. Perhaps the most important cognitive factor for Joseph is his one and only reason for living, his dog, Bandit, who he loves very much. While supporting this reason for living, the therapist may also at the same time examine and expand the suicide fantasy, namely what Bandit would do and feel if the dog found him dead, and what would happen to her after he was gone (e.g., taken to a kennel, put to sleep, etc.). The use of this reason for living may eventually tie in to developing a larger life purpose, and perhaps result in Joseph meeting other people who use dog therapy to help others and involve Bandit in such a program(**Interpersonal Systems**).

The psychotherapy relationship once again is the power source where such interventions can be offered and accepted by the person on the dark journey. Joseph is desperately in need of an intimate, accepting relationship whereby the therapist validates his dark journey and why suicide has come to be the only escape from a terribly painful, uncontrollable existence.

Fortunately, Joseph has one important reason for living, which the therapist can use and fortify. To deepen the therapeutic relationship (and perhaps facilitate it becoming another important reason for living), the therapist may want to invite Bandit to some therapy sessions and allow the dog to become part of the therapeutic relationship, the part that has and will continue to be a reason and hope for Joseph surviving the dark journey. Bandit needs him and he needs Bandit. Keeping his depression in check by taking his medication, attending AA and maintaining sobriety, and working on himself insures he will be there to take care of her.

9

Risk Management and the Dark Journey

As discussed in previous chapters, the psychotherapist's work with the suicidal person on the dark journey is intense, provokes anxiety, and is often depressing. Moreover, the ethical responsibility the therapist has to accurately assess, treat, and protect the person from suicide can be haunting and sometimes overwhelming. Added to this personal struggle of the therapist is the reality that suicide is one the most common malpractice claims brought against psychotherapists (Bongar, 2002; Barnett & Porter, 1998). As a result, some psychotherapists try to avoid or minimize the work, and others focus much of their attention on practicing defensively. I can think of no better example than the one used previously of the psychologist in private practice who exclaimed, "Don't deal with suicide! It's a cop-out! About something else! Not gonna' reward a patient for suicide!" Practicing defensively often takes the form of excessive documentation, excessive use (and cost) of testing measures, and over consulting or over referring, all of which may not reflect actual good care and practice with the suicidal person.

I have been amazed in recent years at the number of books, articles, and training seminars that teach risk management "systems" without addressing the value, integrity, and quality of the psychotherapeutic relationship. Good risk management and documentation are all about the therapist taking good care of the person with the suicide ideas who suffers on the dark journey.

Successful suicide malpractice claims generally involve poor care of the suicidal person, which falls into the following categories from Jobes & Berman (1993, p. 92).

1) Failure to diagnose and safeguard

2) Failure to recognize a patient's suicidal tendencies and not take precautionary measures to protect the patient

3) Failure to use proper care and treatment

To provide good care, the therapist should know exactly what the clinical and legal standards of care are in working with the suicidal person. He or she should regularly attend advanced training in working with suicidal people, especially in light of the fact that most graduate training programs lack formalized training in clinical suicidology. The therapist should also seek consultation when unsure or when the person is not moving away from the dark journey. The American Association of Suicidology has a clinical division which can be used as a reference and consultation source (202-237-2280). He or she should of course have appropriate liability insurance coverage for his or her professional practice. All therapists working with the suicidal person should have Bruce Bongar's (2002) *The Suicidal Patient: Clinical and Legal Standards of Care* in their library, which is the state of the art, classic text in suicide risk management.

For our purposes, I have provided a simple, easy to remember model of risk management, called **B.E. S.M.A.R.T.** Specifically, the factors of **B**lindness, **E**mpathy, **S**tage, **M**odality, **A**lternatives, **R**isk Level, and **T**reatment will be considered.

Blindness is a critical mental factor for assessment, intervention, and risk management for the suicidal person. The suicidal person's mind is dark and blind to alternative solutions/coping responses, reasons for living, and hope. This darkness (blindness) varies in degree depending upon the dark suicide ideas, the dark emotions, dark physiology, and the psychache threshold. In deciding to provide psychotherapy to the suicidal person and referring the person to alternative therapies (e.g., psychiatric evaluation and treatment, partial day hospitalization, hospitalization, and the development of safety nets), the psychotherapist must have a clear sense of the person's level of darkness. The record should reflect this assessment, the rationale for chosen interventions, the reasons for making referrals to other treatment providers, and the safety nets used. Ongoing assessment of this mental blindness is important in the course of therapy to determine treatment impact and whether the treatment plan is in need of revision.

Empathy is a core theme of the psychotherapeutic relationship with the suicidal person. It should guide the therapist in decision making, treatment planning, and/or referrals to or consultations with alternative treatment providers. The record should reflect the therapist's understanding of the suicide idea from the person's point of view and provide estimates of the person's suicide risk level at different points in time. The therapist will develop, implement, and modify the treatment plan based on this empathetic understanding of the person's suicide idea and dark journey. Good person care and good risk management direct the therapist to use as many data sources as possible in developing this understanding, including a review of previous records, interviews with current and past treatment providers, and interviews with family members and significant others. The record should outline these effort and the data obtained.

Another important function of empathy in risk management is to extend this understanding and compassion to the family and significant others of the suicidal person. As much as the person allows, family members and friends should be an integral part of the treatment plan, to include providing safety nets for the suicidal person during times of crisis or dyscontrol. The experience of the dark journey for loved ones must be recognized and validated. It is a very stressful, anxious journey to live and care for a suicidal person. In the event the person actually commits suicide, the therapist should not retreat but rather expand outreach to the grieving family. The therapist should educate loved ones about the suicide-survivor grief reaction and try to get them hooked into a support group. The American Association of Suicidology has a national suicide survivor network that can provide education and counseling to the family members and lead them to a support group in their area (202-237-2280). In addition to helping people who have suffered greatly with the dark journey and death of the deceased, this outreach goes a long way in preventing malpractice claims, which often come about because of the family's anger toward and alienation from the victim's therapist.

The **S**tage of the suicide idea is also critically important in risk management. Determining how far along a person has progressed in the suicide process will determine the level of interventions, suicide precautions, and need for hospitalization of the suicidal person. The person's history in the suicide stages is also very important in decision making. As a person repeatedly moves through the suicide stages, and the more advanced the stage and the suicide intention, with planning and dyscontrol, the greater the risk is for eventual suicide. The record should reflect this assessment currently and historically for the suicidal person. As noted earlier, there are structured, standardized instruments to measure these stages and help the therapist estimate suicide risk. Generally, outpatient psychotherapy is most appropriate for people at the stages of passive suicide ideation, suicide contemplation, and suicide planning and decision making (as long as the person's controls are intact and he or she is willing and able to enter into a pro-living relationship agreement with safety nets established). In addition, rapid employment of treatment interventions at Stage 3 to reduce emotional suffering and fortify controls is necessary. For the person approaching the psychache threshold, especially with a history of previous dyscontrol and suicide actions, the suicide precautions and interventions needed to protect the person are usually beyond the scope that can be provided in outpatient psychotherapy.

The record should note the suicide stage, the history of stage progression, and the levels of controls the suicidal person has. Based on this assessment, appropriate stage-level interventions and/or referrals should be provided, along with the rationale for these decisions. It should be noted that for cases in need of interventions beyond the scope available in psychotherapy, the therapist is responsible not only for the referral but for insuring that the appropriate follow-up occurs, including contacting the referral source, involving the family in the referral process, and sometimes (e.g., in a suicide crisis) even taking the person to the provider or hospital. The record must outline all of these steps of intervention, referral, and follow-up to insure there is no appearance or occurrence of abandonment.

Modality refers to the multiple biopsychosocial systems operating in the suicide idea and dark journey of the person as he or she transacts with negative life stress over time. Lazarus's (1995) multimodal scheme of **B.A.S.I.C. I.D.** is a very useful guide for the therapist in identifying all relevant systems of the suicidal person in the assessment. It also provides a logical extension of the assessment to intervention targets for the suicidal person. Most modalities are amenable to psychotherapeutic intervention. The record should reflect what is being done, why it is being done, and how it ties in to the multimodal assessment. Follow-up modality assessment will help demonstrate the efficacy of the interventions provided or needed to modify the treatment plan—all of which should be noted in the record. Finally, in terms of the Sensations and Drugs modalities, when indicated, the therapist, if not a psychiatrist, should refer the person for psychiatric treatment with the use of psychotropic medication to reduce affective symptoms and elevate the psychache threshold. This referral should be noted in the record as well as the therapist's follow-up with the referral source. If improvement is not seen, the therapist will want to again contact the provider to advise him or her of this status so that he or she may modify treatment as warranted. The record should outline all of these steps.

Alternatives—the therapist must appreciate psychotherapy as one avenue among many to help the suicidal person retreat from the dark journey. A variety of other interventions may be indicated based on the multimodal assessment, to include marital/family therapy, medical examination/treatment (in the event there is an underlying physiological disorder contributing to the dark journey, such as thyroid disease), social services, vocational training, pastoral/spiritual counseling, psychiatric medication treatment, psychiatric hospitalization, and E.C.T. Even when it comes to psychotherapy, sometimes a person will work with one therapist better than another. The therapist should be open to all possibilities of relief for the dark journey and support these pursuits, while establishing a backup plan and safety nets should these prove ineffective.

The record should reflect the rationale and use for alternative interventions, the therapist's follow-up to these interventions, and the development of a relapse plan for the suicidal person should the dark journey worsen or return. The suicidal person should be encouraged to anticipate what might happen, how he or she might feel, and what suicide thoughts might return in the future that would indicate the person should resume psychotherapy. The nature of the dark journey and the suicide idea is that it often repeats itself and the person needs to expect, anticipate, and prepare for this likely possibility. The therapist likewise should make periodic phone call checkups with the person to see how he or she is doing. The record reflects that ongoing concern for the person represents good therapeutic care and good risk management.

Risk level estimation is a constant process during the course of therapy. This estimation is based on the presence of the suicide idea, its progression and stage, and the dark journey and varying **B.A.S.I.C. I.D.** transactions of the person with life stress over time. Unlike prediction, which is an unobtainable goal (Pokorny, 1993), risk estimation provides periodic snapshots of the person, at a given stage, with varying **B.A.S.I.C. I.D.** vulnerabilities or risk factors. Risk level can be categorized as low, moderate, or high based on this snapshot, which should directly influence treatment planning, suicide precautions, and safety networks. People at Stage 1 of passive suicide ideation or Stage 2 of suicide contemplation are likely to be assigned a low to moderate suicide risk level and are relatively safe within the outpatient psychotherapy model. The person who has advanced to Stage 3 and has made the decision to commit suicide, has thought of the plan and method, is unwilling to enter into a pro-living relationship agreement, is hopeless, has poor controls as the result of substance abuse or a serotonin deficiency, and has a personal and family history of suicide attempts would be estimated at a high risk for suicide action. Immediate crisis stabilization, suicide precautions, and likely hospitalization would be called for. The record should reflect all of the steps and actions the therapist took to protect this person from suicidal action.

Finally, **T**reatment refers to all the various interventions provided to target the multiple modalities of the suicide idea and the dark journey. The therapeutic relationship is the power source for the success of such interventions as it provides hope and reasons for living in the midst of despair and engages the suicidal person to try and trust these interventions to provide relief and reverse the dark journey. The field has advanced to the point that specific types of interventions have been demonstrated to be effective in reducing suicidality, and are considered the standard of care. Therapists will want to use some forms of cognitive therapy for the **Cognitive/Images Modalities** and dialectical behavior therapy for the **Behavior/Affect Modalities**. Pharmacological interventions will also often be appropriate to target the **Sensations/ Drugs Modalities**, namely to reduce emotional suffering and improve psychache threshold. The record should reflect this multimodal approach and the rationale for selected interventions.

In conclusion, the **B.E. S.M.A.R.T.** model offers a simplistic, multimodal, data-based guide for the therapist in providing relationship care, appropriate stage/modality-specific interventions, risk management, and documentation.

10

Taking Care of the Psychotherapist on the Dark Journey

The personal, professional, and ethical struggles of being a psychotherapist taking care of people in great need has been addressed (Bonner, 2005c; Saakvitne, 2002). Psychotherapists are viewed as high risk for burnout as a result of their work. Specifically, clinicians at risk for burnout tend to be highly dedicated and committed to their clients, struggle with inner pressure to accomplish and succeed, and experience intense internal and external pressure to serve the needs of people who suffer from overwhelming problems (Grosh & Olsen, 1995). There is no greater problem for the psychotherapist than the life-death struggle of people with the suicide idea who are on a dark journey of unbearable emotional pain. Joining the person on the dark journey provokes anxiety, depression, and exhaustion. The added stress of ethical and legal standards, risk management, and liability all weigh heavily on psychotherapists. It would seem to me that psychotherapists who work with suicidal people are most at risk for burnout and emotional suffering, given the nature of the work. Therapists should have a proactive plan of self-care in place to replenish emotional energy, avoid undue suffering, prevent burnout, and protect themselves from developing their own dark journey of the suicidal mind, which is a real possibility.

The scheme of **H.E.A.L.T.H.** will be offered as a guide to the therapist in taking care of himself or herself. Specifically, the factors of **Heal-**

ing, **E**xistential Meaning, **A**ltruism, **L**ight, **T**rust, and **H**ope will be considered.

The psychotherapist is a healer of the dark journey and is in need of healing from the dark journey. Many psychotherapists come into this work as a result of their own unmet needs, hurts, and pains of living. These characteristics are useful in the sense that they better sensitize the therapist to understand and validate the person's dark journey. However, the therapist must have others in his or her life who care deeply, can validate his or her dark journey, and provide outlets for relief and recovery. Psychotherapy for the psychotherapist is an important avenue to pursue for this healing.

In addition to what the psychotherapist brings to this work, the work itself, as previously noted, is anxiety-ridden and often depressing. Joining a person on the dark journey entails a psychological transformation whereby the therapist sees and feels from the mind of the suicidal person. This transformation can profoundly affect the therapist and move him or her toward the dark journey and the person's way of thinking. It is good for therapists to work with other types of clients who are dealing with more positive, growth-oriented aspects of living. In addition, pursuing more immediately reinforcing types of work can be good therapy for the therapist, including teaching, consultation, professional writing, and research. The therapist needs a well-balanced professional and personal life that brings good experiences, emotional outlets, love, and intimacy.

The most significant, devastating risk in working with suicidal people is the possibility of an eventual suicide. This is a tremendous loss to the therapist who has invested almost totally in doing everything that is possible to reverse the suicide idea and dark journey and relieve the emotional suffering of the victim. Feelings of survivor grief and paralyzing feelings of guilt often color the suicide experience for the psychotherapist. The suicidal person trusted you to see and feel the anguish and pain of the dark journey and you were unsuccessful in helping this person recover. The harsh reality of possible litigation only compounds these feelings. The therapist should seek counsel from a supportive colleague who knows the experience personally and, if necessary, seek grief counseling. Participating in suicide survivor support groups as well as accessing the literature on survivors can also be helpful.

Existential meaning is an important healing factor for the suicidal person. The therapist as role-model should emulate a life that has meaning and purpose beyond events and temporary emotions. Most psychotherapists have an overriding set of core beliefs, or a life philosophy, that values human potential, the goodness of life, helping others, and trying to make the world a better place. The wonderful, almost miraculous drive to be a psychotherapist is that you make a difference to people that are hurting. For one faith's tradition, the idea that "what you do to the least of these you do unto me" captures the goodness of the healer's life and work.

Similar to existential meaning, the psychotherapist should remain mindful of what and who drew him or her to the psychotherapy work. It was far more than professional status, intrigue, or pay. The attraction was a profound drive to help suffering people by developing a deeply, caring relationship that offers the best treatments available. If the psychotherapist is overburdened with risk management, managed care, liability, overworks himself or herself, and has personal stressors and strains, he or she is unable to give of himself or herself to the suicidal person on the dark journey. Sometimes we need to step back and have a wake-up call to remember what truly brought us to this work. If this meaning has become shortsighted, the therapist should consider pursuing therapy and may have to decide whether he or she is still able and wants to do this type of potentially all-consuming work.

As noted in earlier chapters, the psychotherapist becomes a beacon of light to the suicidal person who is in the life cave of never-ending darkness. The therapist must be able to see beyond the darkness to alternative paths and methods of relief. The therapist must be willing and able to take the suicidal person's hand and confidently guide him or her out of the dark mental cave into light. While there are a variety of effective modality interventions, it is the psychotherapeutic relationship that engenders hope and light to pursue such strategies. The psychotherapist must envision light, alternatives, possibilities, and hope in the darkest of times. Reality-based optimism, personal hardiness, resilient coping, and access to reasons for living all combine to make the person of the therapist a person of light. When the therapist has lost this vision or the future is cloudy, the therapist should seek professional guidance and reevaluate his or her calling to work with the suicidal person. The concept of therapist as light is critically important for the care of the suicidal person, who day in and day out suffers from a very cold darkness.

Trust is the cornerstone of the therapeutic relationship, one in which the suicidal person comes to trust the therapist as a source of light and relief, and the therapist trusts the person to be honest and committed to a pro-living relationship treatment plan. Beyond the darkness, the psychotherapist must have an overall trust in life and that many times the good outweighs the bad, healing overcomes sickness, and that light and hope overcome darkness and despair. Certainly the therapist needs to be realistic that this is not always the case and there are no guarantees in living, but there is a trust that much of the time things will work out better than not. If the psychotherapist loses this sense of trust or becomes too burdened by the dark journey, he or she should seek out professional guidance and therapy, and decide whether or not he or she can be a source of trust for the suicidal person.

Finally and perhaps most importantly, hope is the essential element for a person to give up the suicide idea and retreat from the dark journey. The person of the therapist comes to represent hope for the suicidal person. Many times the suicidal person will come to depend upon and cling to the therapist as his or her only hope for getting better, seeing possibilities, and building a life worth living. The therapist must be a person of hope both in and out of therapy. The therapist must believe that despite how bad things may seem and feel, one day things are going to get better. This vital life source should be embedded in the therapist's psyche, with a fundamental belief that beyond circumstances, available knowledge, and emotional pain there is a larger belief and value system. This system captures a spiritual essence that life has hope and purpose beyond self that, most of the time, can move people out of the darkness into a purpose-driven, hope-filled life.

11

The Final Chapter of the Dark Journey

The paradox of the last chapter of the dark journey is that most of the time it is not the final chapter. People on the dark journey of the suicidal mind who get better tend to revisit the dark journey when certain life stressors reoccur or their psychache threshold is being pressed. For many, the dark journey becomes a conditioned coping pattern that is reinforced and maintained when one of the dark components resurfaces and triggers the suicide idea (e.g., dark suicide ideas, dark emotions, dark physiology, psychache, life stress, and problems of living).

As a result of this tendency, the psychotherapist must address this nature and teach relapse-prevention skills, to include anticipating and preparing for likely triggers that might reactivate the dark journey, developing a plan of action to reverse this course, and having a repertoire of coping responses to effectively turn around on the dark journey, which should always include the option of returning to psychotherapy. It is a good idea for the therapist to periodically check in with the person after terminating psychotherapy to see how he or she is doing. There should always be an open door to return to the therapeutic relationship for a "booster" session now and again. Relapsing should be reframed as a natural occurrence when habitual patterns are redirected, something to expect and to be prepared for by early intervention and quick turn around. It is very important that the person does not interpret relapse as a bad event indicative of his or her failure to succeed in turning around on the dark journey. Such an interpretation is likely to activate all the previous suicide cognitions and reinforce the notion that the person is a failure. Educating suicidal people about these possibilities before they happen will reroute their thinking to make appropriate, reality-based appraisals of the event and their control in reversing course.

Another consideration in the final chapter of the dark journey for suicide prevention is the overwhelming fact that more than 90 percent of suicides in all age groups are related to mental or addictive disorders (Moscicki, 1995). Society continues to need education and public policy that recognizes mental illness as a potentially life-threatening disorder, an illness for which there are often very effective treatments available today (Barlow, 2004). If people on the dark journey of the suicide idea were treated with the available methods that clear thought and perception, improve mood and controls, reverse addictive behaviors, and raise the psychache threshold, then the risk for completed suicide would be diminished substantially.

However, it still remains the case that most people who suffer mental or addictive disorders do not enter the dark journey of the suicide idea and do not go on to successfully complete suicide. There are unique biopsychosocial person-environment transactions that lend themselves to the dark journey and the suicide idea. Much of what has been covered in previous chapters outlined some of these components and ways to assess and intervene by suicide stage and modality. One area worthy of future attention, first conceptualized by Marsha Linehan's research team (Linehan et al., 1983), is the concept of personal strengths, adaptive beliefs, or reasons for living that motivate people to tolerate emotional pain and provide purpose and meaning to life. These "protectors" seem to be missing for the suicidal person.

The focus on human strengths in the midst of adversity has recently been given much research attention and has even been formally named, defined, and classified as "Positive Psychology" (Peterson & Seligman, 2004). What exactly is it about people who face stress, problems of living, and emotional suffering who do not enter the dark journey of the suicide idea and press toward their psychache threshold? Social problem solving has been cited as a skill strength that makes life meaningful and promotes personal growth and development (Chang, D'Zurilla, & Sanna, 2004). Characterological strengths of resilient coping and flourishing have been proposed, to include creativity, curiosity, open-mindedness, hardiness, love of learning, perspective, bravery, persistence, integrity, vitality, love, kindness, social intelligence, citizenship, fairness, leadership, forgiveness and mercy, modesty and humility, prudence, self-regulation, appreciation of beauty and excellence, gratitude, hope, humor, and spirituality. (Aspinwall & Staudinger, 2003; Keyes & Haidt, 2003; Lopez & Snyder, 2003; Peterson & Seligman, 2004). Others have articulated that satisfaction of the primary psychological needs for affiliation, endurance, generation, and nurturing protect the person from the strains and stressors of life and facilitate positive, life-enhancing coping (Shneidman, 2001). Still others have articulated the importance of the "life well lived,"which fortifies adaptive, life-oriented coping, whereby goodness transcends self through the arts, nature, children, intimacy, family, work, social causes, volunteerism, community, and faith (Keyes & Haidt, 2003; Seneca (4BC–69AD) cited in Shneidman, 2001).

All of these areas represent potentially ripe territory for the suicidal person to explore and develop. Ultimately, building a life that has purpose and meaning beyond the present provides light down the road or in the bigger picture for the person on the dark journey of the suicidal mind. Psychotherapists should teach, support, and facilitate growth in these areas, which in the long run may come to protect the suicidal person from overwhelming darkness, intolerable emotional pain, and despair. Having a purpose-driven life gives a person reasons to live and goals to strive for beyond temporary moments of darkness and pain.

A psychotherapist's dark journey into the suicidal mind is difficult and complex, varying by stages, modalities, and biopsychosocial person-environment transactions. There are numerous assessment and intervention targets, measurements, and techniques that the psychotherapist can use to reverse the journey. There is also a host of recently identified and clarified skills, strengths, and protectors that can mitigate the dark suicide journey and light the way for hope, purpose, and meaning beyond disturbing events, thoughts, and emotions. Ultimately, it is the relationship between the psychotherapist and the suicidal person that validates the dark journey and builds the bridge to such possibilities. The father of American suicidology, Dr. Edwin Shneidman, most eloquently captured the essence of good psychotherapy after reviewing all of the major works on suicide in the twentieth century. It is this message that fully brings the final chapter of the dark journey of the suicide idea to an end.

> Regrettably, I believe that all of the demographic studies
> from Enrico Morselli (through Emile Durkheim, Maurice
> Halbwachs—19th century European "suicidologists"—and
> this year's dissertations) on; all the biochemical work,
> through the elegant laboratory experiments; all the
> important psychological and psychiatric papers cited
> by Maltsberger and Goldblatt (my own included); all
> the poignant confessionals about manic-depressive
> disorder are, at their best, background hum or music.
> But music, hum, or noise, they are background. They
> fail to address the necessary cause of suicide—
> as opposed to their focus on different kinds of perturbations (e.g.,
> depression)
> or concomitants of suicide (e.g., social status or biochemical markers).
> For me, today, still the core data to elicit from
> a potentially suicidal person are not a family history, a spinal
> tap assay, a demographic survey, a psychiatric account, a
> psychodynamic interview, or a self-report of a mental illness, but
> rather—keeping all of these relevant bits of information in mind—

what is directly to the suicidal person's point, namely
a full anamnestic response to the two basic questions in clinical suicidology:
"Where do you hurt?" and "How may I help you?"

—(Shneidman, 2001, p. 203).

Note: From *Comprehending Suicide* by Edwin S. Shneidman, 2001.
Copyright by the American Psychological Association. Reprinted by
permission of the author and publisher.

References

Aspinwall, L., & Staudinger, U. (2003). *The psychology of human strengths: Fundamental questions and future directions for a positive psychology.* Washington, DC: American Psychological Association.

Barlow, D.K. (2004). Psychological treatments. <u>American Psychologist</u>, <u>59(9)</u>, 869–878.

Barnett, J.E., & Porter, J.E. (1998). The suicidal patient: Clinical and risk management strategies. In L. VandeCreek, S. Knapp, & T. Jackson (Eds), *Innovations in clinical practice: A source book* (Vol. 16, pp. 95–108). Sarasota, FL: Professional Resource Exchange.

Beck, A.T. (1996). Beyond belief: A theory of modes, personality, and psychopathology. In P. Salkovskis (Ed.), *Frontiers of cognitive therapy* (pp. 1–25). New York: Guilford.

Beck, A.T. (1986). Hopelessness as a predictor of eventual suicide. In J. Mann & M. Stanley (Eds.), *Psychobiology of suicidal behavior.* New York: Academy of Sciences.

Beck, A.T. (1976). *Cognitive therapy and the emotional disorders.* New York: New American Library.

Beck, A.T., Kovacs, M., & Weissman, A. (1979). Assessment of suicidal intention: The Scale for Suicidal Ideation. <u>Journal of Consulting and Clinical Psychology</u>, <u>47(2)</u>, 343–352.

Beck, A.T., & Lester, D. (1976). Components of suicidal intent in completed and attempted suicide. Journal of Psychology, 92, 35–38.

Beck, A.T., Schuyler, D., & Herman, I. (1974). Development of the suicide intent scale. In A.T. Beck, H.L.P. Resnick, & D.J. Lettieri (Eds), *The prediction of suicide* (pp. 45–56). Bowie, MD: Charles Press.

Beck, A.T., Steer, R.A., & Brown, G. (1993). Dysfunctional attitudes and suicidal ideation in psychiatric outpatients. Suicide and Life-Threatening Behavior, 23(1), 11–20.

Beck, A.T., Steer, R.A., Kovacs, M., & Garrison, B. (1985). Hopelessness and eventual suicide: A prospective study of patients hospitalized with suicidal ideation. American Journal of Psychiatry, 142, 559–563.

Bongar, B. (2002). *The suicidal patient: Clinical and legal standards (Second Edition)*. Washington, DC: American Psychological Association.

Bonner, R.L. (2005c). Occupational hazards of being a mental health provider in corrections. In L. VandeCreek, & J. Allen (Eds.), *Innovations in clinical practice: Focus on health and well-ness*. Sarasota, FL: Professional Resource Exchange.

Bonner, R.L. (2005b). *Stressful conditions, isolated housing, and psychosocial vulnerability in prison suicide ideators: Another test of a process model*. Manuscript under review.

Bonner, R.L. (2005a). *A process approach to suicide prevention behind bars*. Book manuscript under review.

Bonner, R.L. (2001). Moving suicide risk assessment into the next millennium: Lessons from our past. In D. Lester (Ed.), *Suicide prevention: Resources for the new millennium* (pp. 83–103. Philadelphia, PA: Taylor and Francis (Brunner-Routledge).

Bonner, R.L., & Michalik-Bonner, D. (1996). The suicidal patient in private practice: A multimodal approach. Psychotherapy in Private Practice, 14(4), 1–15.

Bonner, R.L., & Rich, A.R. (1992). Cognitive vulnerability and hopelessness among correctional inmates. Journal of Offender Rehabilitation, 17(3/4), 113–122.

Bonner, R.L., & Rich, A.R. (1991). Predicting vulnerability to hopelessness under conditions of negative life stress. The Journal of Nervous and Mental Disease, 179(1), 29–32.

Bonner, R.L., & Rich, A.R. (1988a). A prospective investigation of suicide ideation in college students: A test of a model. Suicide and Life-Threatening Behavior, 18(4), 245–258

Bonner, R.L., & Rich, A.R. (1988b). Negative life stress, social problem solving appraisal, and hopelessness: Implications for suicide research. Cognitive Therapy and Research, 12(6), 849–856.

Bonner, R.L., & Rich, A.R. (1987). Toward a predictive model of suicidal ideation and behavior: Some preliminary data in college students. Suicide and Life-Threatening Behavior, 17(1), 50–63.

Brent, D., Perper, J., Moritz, G., Baugher, M., Roth, C., Balach, L., & Schweers, J. (1993). Stressful life events, psychopathology, and adolescent suicide: A case control study. Suicide and Life-Threatening Behavior, 23(3), 179–187.

Chang, E., D'Zurilla, T., & Sanna, L. (Eds) (2004). *Social problem solving: Theory, research, and training.* Washington, DC: American Psychological Association.

Clum, G.A., Febbraro, G.A.R. (2004). Social problem solving and suicide risk. In E.C. Chang, T.J. D'Zurilla, & L.J. Sanna (Eds.), *Social problem solving: Theory, research, and training* (pp. 67–82). Washington, DC: American Psychological Association.

Cochrane, R., & Robertson, A. (1975). Stress in the lives of parasuiciders. Social Psychiatry, 10, 161–172.

Dixon, W., Rumford, K., Heppner, P., & Lips, B. (1992). Use of different sources of stress to predict hopelessness and suicide ideation in a college population. Journal of Counseling Psychology, 38, 51–56.

D'Zurilla, T.J., Nezu, A.M., & Maydeu-Olivares, A. (2004). Social problem solving: Theory and assessment. In E. Chang, T. D'Zurilla, & L. Sanna (Eds.), *Social problem solving: Theory, research, and training* (pp. 11–28). Washington, DC: American Psychological Association.

Ellis, T.E., & Newman, C.F. (1996). *Choosing to live: How to defeat suicide through cognitive therapy.* Oakland, CA: New Harbinger Publications.

Eyman, J.R., & Eyman, J.K., (1992). Personality assessment in suicide prediction. In R. Maris, A. Berman, J. Maltsberger, & R. Yufit (Eds.), *Assessment and prediction of suicide* (pp. 183–201). New York: Guilford.

Fawcett, J. (1999). Profiles of completed suicides. In D. Jacobs (Ed.), *The Harvard Medical School guide to suicide assessment and intervention* (pp. 115–124). San Francisco, CA: Jossey-Bass.

Frankl, V. (1977). *Man's search for ultimate meaning.* New York: Plenum.

Grosch, W., & Olsen, D. (1995). Therapist burnout: A self psychology and systems perspective. In L. VandeCreek, S. Knapp, & T. Jackson (Eds.), *Innovations in clinical practice* (Vol. 14, pp. 439–454). Sarasota, FL: Professional Resource Exchange.

Guttmacher, L.B. (1994). *Psychopharmacology and electroconvulsive therapy.* Washington, DC: American Psychiatric Press.

Hendin, H. (1993). The suicide of Anne Sexton. Suicide and Life-Threatening Behavior, 23(3), 257–262.

Hendin, H., Maltsberger, J., Haas, A., Szanto, K., & Rabinowicz, H. (2004). Desperation and other affective states in suicidal patients. Suicide and Life-Threatening Behavior, 34(4), 386–394.

Jamison, K. (1999). Suicide and manic depressive illness: An overview. In D. Jacobs (Ed.), *The Harvard Medical School guide to suicide assessment and intervention* (pp. 251–269).San Francisco, CA: Jossey-Bass.

Jobes, D.A., & Berman, A.L. (1993). Suicide and malpractice liability: Assessing and revising policies, procedures, and practice in outpatient settings. Professional Psychology: Research and Practice, 24, 91–99.

Keyes, C., & Haidt, J. (2003). *Flourishing: Positive psychology and the life well-lived.* Washington, DC: American Psychological Association.

King, C.A. (1988). Suicide across the life span: Pathways to prevention. Suicide and Life-Threatening Behavior, 28, 328–337.

Kral, M. (1994). Suicide: A social logic. Suicide and Life-Threatening Behavior, 24, 245–255.

Lazarus, A.A. (1995). Multimodal therapy. In R.J. Corsini, & D. Wedding (Eds.), *Current psychotherapies*, 5th edition (pp. 322–355). Itasca, IL: Peacock.

Linehan, M.M. (1999). Standard protocol of assessing and treating suicidal behavior for patients in treatment. In D.G. Jacobs (Ed.), *The Harvard Medical School guide to suicide assessment and intervention* (pp. 146–187). San Francisco, CA: Jossey Bass.

Linehan, M.M. (1987) Dialectical behavior therapy for borderline personality disorder. Bulletin of the Menninger Clinic, 51, 261–276

Linehan, M. (1985). Reasons for living inventory. In P.A. Keller, & L.G. Ritt (Eds.), *Innovations in clinical practice* (Vol. 4, pp. 321–330). Sarasota, FL: Professional Resource Exchange.

Linehan, M.M., Camper, P., Chiles, J., Strosahl, K., & Shearin, E. (1987). Interpersonal problem-solving and parasuicide. Cognitive Therapy and Research, 11, 1–12.

Linehan, M.M., Goodstein, J., Nielsen, S., & Chiles, J. (1983). Reasons for staying alive when you think of killing yourself: The reasons for living inventory. Journal of Consulting and Clinical Psychology, 51, 276–286.

Lopez, S., & Snyder, C. (Eds.) (2003) *Positive psychological assessment: A handbook of models and measures*. Washington, DC: American Psychological Association.

Luscomb, R., Clum, G.A., & Patsiokas, A.T. (1980). Mediating factors in the relationship between life stress and suicide attempts. Journal of Nervous and Mental Disease, 168, 644–649.

Maltsberger, J.T., & Buie, D.H. (1973). Countertransference hate in the treatment of suicidal patients. Archives of General Psychiatry, 30, 625–633.

Mann, J., & Arango, V. (1999). The neurobiology of suicidal behavior. In D. Jacobs (Ed.), *The Harvard Medical School Guide to suicide assessment and intervention* (pp. 98–114). San Francisco, CA: Jossey-Bass.

Medina, J. (1998). *Depression: How it happens, how it's healed*. Oakland, CA: New Harbinger Publications.

Moscicki, E.K. (1995). Epidemiology of suicidal behavior. Suicide and Life-Threatening Behavior, 25(1), 22–35.

Paykel, E., Prusoff, B., & Myers, J. (1975). Suicide attempts and recent life events. Archives of General Psychiatry, 32, 327–333.

Peterson, C., & Seligman, M. (2004). *Character strengths and virtues: A handbook and classification*. Washington, DC: American Psychological Association.

Pokorny, A.D. (1993). Suicide prediction revisited. Suicide and Life-Threatening Behavior, 23(1), 1–10.

Quinnett, P.G. (1997). *Suicide: The forever decision*. New York: The Crossroad Publishing Company.

Rich, A.R., & Bonner, R.L. (1990). *A process model of suicidal behavior*. Indiana, PA: Indiana University of Pennsylvania.

Roy, A. (2001). Psychiatric treatment in suicide prevention. In D. Lester (Ed.), *Suicide prevention: Resources for the millennium* (pp. 103–128). Philadelphia, PA: Taylor & Francis (Brunner-Routledge).

Roy, A. (1992). Genetics, biology, and suicide in the family. In R. Maris, A. Berman, J. Maltsberger, & R. Yufit (Eds.), *Assessment and prediction of suicide* (pp. 574–585). New York: Guilford.

Rudd, M.D., Joiner, T., & Rajab, M.H. (2001). *Treating suicidal behavior: An effective, time-limited approach.* New York: Guilford.

Rudd, M.D., Rajab, M.H., & Dahm, P. (1994). Problem-solving appraisal in suicide ideators and attempters. American Journal of Orthopsychiatry, 64, 136–149.

Saakvitne, K.W. (2002). How to avoid occupational hazards of being a psychotherapist. In L. VandeCreek, & T. Jackson (Eds.), *Innovations in clinical practice* (Vol. 20, pp. 325–340). Sarasota, FL: Professional Resource Exchange.

Salzman, C. (1999). Treatment of the suicidal patient with psychotropic drugs and ECT. In D. Jacobs (Ed.), *The Harvard Medical School Guide to suicide assessment and intervention* (pp. 372–382). San Francisco, CA: Jossey-Bass Publishers.

Schotte, D.E., & Clum, G.A. (1987). Problem-solving skills in suicidal psychiatric patients. Journal of Consulting and Clinical Psychology, 55, 49–54.

Schotte, D.E., & Clum, G.A. (1982). Suicide ideation in a college population: A test of a model. Journal of Consulting and Clinical Psychology, 50, 690–696.

Shneidman, E. (2005). How do I read. Suicide and Life-Threatening Behavior, 35(2), 117–120.

Shneidman, E. (2004). *Autopsy of a Suicidal Mind.* New York: Oxford Press.

Shneidman, E. (2001). *Comprehending suicide*. Washington, DC: American Psychological Association.

Shneidman, E. (1999). The psychological pain assessment scale. <u>Suicide and Life-Threatening Behavior</u>, <u>29</u>, 287–294.

Shneidman, E. (1993). *Suicide as psychache: A clinical approach to self-destructive behavior*. Northvale, NJ: Aronson.

Shneidman, E.S. (1998). Further reflections on suicide as psychache. <u>Suicide and Life-Threatening-Behavior</u>, <u>28</u>, 245–250.

VanderKolk, B., Perry, C., & Herman, J.L. (1991). Childhood origins of self-destructive behavior. <u>American Journal of Psychiatry</u>, <u>148</u>, 1165–1671.

Van Pragg, H. (2001). Suicide and aggression: Are they biologically two sides of the same coin? In D. Lester (Ed.), *Suicide prevention: Resources for the millennium* (pp. 45–60). Philadelphia, PA: Taylor and Francis (Brunner-Routledge).

Warman, D.M., Forman, E.M., Henriques, G.R., Brown, G.K., & Beck, A.T. (2004). Suicidality and psychosis: Beyond depression and hopelessness. <u>Suicide and Life-Threatening Behavior</u>, <u>34(1)</u>, 77–86.

Weishaar, M.E., & Beck, A.T. (1992). Clinical and cognitive predictors of suicide. In R. Maris, A. Berman, J. Maltsberger, & R. Yufit (Eds.), *Assessment and prediction of suicide* (pp. 467–483). New York: Guilford.

Weiss, R., & Hufford, M. (1999). Substance abuse and suicide. In D. Jacobs (Ed.), *The Harvard Medical School Guide to suicide assessment and intervention* (pp. 300–310). San Francisco, CA: Jossey-Bass.

Yang, B., & Clum, G.A. (1996). Effects of early negative life experiences on cognitive functioning and risk for suicide: A review. Clinical Psychology Review, 16, 177–195.

Yufit, R.I., & Bongar, B. (1992). Suicide, stress, and coping with life cycle events. In R. Maris, A. Berman, J. Maltsberger, & R. Yufit (Eds.), *Assessment and prediction of suicide* (pp. 553–573). New York: Guilford.

About the Author

Ronald L. Bonner, Psy.D., is a clinical psychologist who has worked with suicidal people in inpatient and outpatient settings, jails and prisons, and private practice over the past eighteen years. His research interests include clinical suicidology and depression. Dr. Bonner has presented his research to numerous national and international professional meetings and has authored or co-authored about fifty publications. He is currently the Chief Psychologist at the Federal Correctional Institution-Allenwood and serves as a consulting editor for *Suicide and Life-Threatening Behavior*. Dr. Bonner lives in the country with his wife, Diane, who is a child clinical psychologist, and his two rowdy sons, Jason and Joshua, who give him all the reasons for living, positive energy, and exhaustion that an old man can stand.

**Dr. Bonner may be contacted at Three South Market Street, Selinsgrove, PA, 17870, (570) 374-4305 (e-mail: rbonner@bop.gov). The views expressed in this work are solely those of the author and do not necessarily represent any of his institutional or organizational affiliations.

978-0-595-35484-9
0-595-35484-X

www.ingramcontent.com/pod-product-compliance
Lightning Source LLC
Chambersburg PA
CBHW030405290526
45785CB00004B/1908